Inter-City meeting
Jan 14, 1991 —

In appreciation

Bob Taylor
Reno Kottas
Cal Class "66"

# RENO
## THE PAST REVISITED

is dedicated to the
Seventy-fifth Anniversary
of the
Greater Reno-Sparks
Chamber of Commerce
and the individuals
who over the years
have made it successful.

Bill Wallace
Chamber President
1988

THE CHAMBER
75 YEARS OF PROGRESS
1913–1988
Diamond Jubilee

# RENO
## THE PAST REVISITED

### NORM NIELSON

THE
DONNING COMPANY
PUBLISHERS
NORFOLK / VIRGINIA BEACH

Design by Sharon V. Moyer

The Donning Company/Publishers
5659 Virginia Beach Boulevard
Norfolk, Virginia 23502

Edited by Joanna Maddron
Richard A. Horwege, Senior Editor

**Library of Congress Cataloging-in-Publication Data**

Nielson, Norm, 1944-
    Reno: the past revisited/by Norm Nielson.
        p.    cm.
    Bibliography: p.
    Includes index.
    ISBN 0-89865-742-3 (lim. ed.)
    1. Reno (Nev.)—History—Pictorial works. 2. Reno (Nev.)—
Description—Views. I. Title.
F849.R4N55      1988                                    88-29970
979.3'55'0222—dc 19                                    CIP

**Printed in the United States of America**

# Contents

# Preface

*"I have put all that I had to say into the body of this book; but being informed that a preface is a necessary evil... I have written this one."*

Norm Nielson
Stolen from Comstock author
Dan DeQuille

# Acknowledgments

The Reno/Sparks area is one that the Chamber of Commerce is proud to have served over the past seventy-five years. It is challenging to be associated with a strong and caring community that demands quality in both its recreation and business activities. We feel extremely fortunate to have had the opportunity to prepare this pictorial history book for you and demonstrate our spirit and pride in Reno and Sparks.

We express our deepest appreciation to those who assisted us in the preparation of *Reno: The Past Revisited*, including those community members who provided us with cherished photographs of the past and present.

Ron Watson, Chamber Executive Vice President
Patti Pietsch, Public Relations Director
Norm Nielson, Author
Mark Savage, Photography

Phil Earl, Nevada Historical Society
Cyndee Privitt, Administrative Assistant
Jane Bechtel, Administrative Assistant
Cyndi Fleiner, Marketing Coordinator

*Photo donors:*
John Ascuaga's Nugget; Edwin Bender; Frank Bender/Bender Warehouse; Bennett photos; Frances Brisbin; Ralph Casazza/Tore Ltd. Shoppers Square; Neal Cobb; Bob Davis/Media Consultants/Dermody Properties; Geneviev Desautel; Greater Reno-Sparks Chamber of Commerce; Jean C. Hubbard; the Kleppe family; Arma McCusker; Harvey M. Moll; Nevada Bell; Nevada Historical Society; the Harry O'Brien family; Roy Powers; Reno News Bureau; Reno Orthopedic Clinic; Reno-Sparks Convention and Visitors Authority; St. Mary's Regional Medical Center; Mark Savage; Sparks Heritage Foundation and Museum; Frank M. Steinheimer; University of California-Berkeley, Bancroft Library; Ross Wainwright; and Ethel Warren.

# Introduction

*"The fact is that Reno, though a neat and pretty town,
with one of those western situations that break the eastern heart with envy,
is a very dull town for the visitor."*

Katherine Geroald
*The Aristocratic West,* 1925

Reno, dull?

Our town has been called many things. It has been called sinful, like Sodom and Gomorrah, a town tainted by divorce and ruled by the corruption of gambling. It has been called rustic, backwards almost, a place where cowhands fresh from the range wander through plush casinos without wiping their boots. And though surrounded by desert, Reno has even been called "beautiful" and "a city of trembling leaves." But dull? Never!

And no wonder. This city, though still in its infancy, has seen it all—the rich and the famous, the gallant and the gangster. From Mary Pickford to Baby Face Nelson, from Marilyn Monroe to the President of the United States, Reno, Nevada, has come a long way.

If you are expecting this pictorial to be just a glowing account of Reno's rich heritage, you might as well return this book to the shelf. Reno, like most cities, has had its share of crime, crooked politicians, mismanagement, and bad publicity, and these events will be included here as well. Remember, warts, though ugly to some, can be interesting to others—warts are, after all, a fact of life.

As this book nears completion in the spring of 1988, Reno is about to change dramatically. Gone are the Mapes and the Riverside. No longer do we hear the cry of "Harold's Club or Bust!" The city faces financial problems of monumental proportions, yet major casinos are expanding, the new Riverboat is open, and the downtown core is undergoing a much-needed facelift. The city is dangerously short of police officers. Schoolteachers' salaries still remain surprisingly low. While residents question the viability of further growth, pollution counts are up, airport noise increases, and the Convention Center struggles to expand. Meanwhile, we are about to experience the second-worst drought in recorded history.

So on this, the seventy-fifth anniversary of the Greater Reno-Sparks Chamber of Commerce, this book becomes a history of a city at the crossroads. It is a small town perhaps, as yet unfulfilled. Still, it remains the place we have come to call, with some boast and no small amount of pride, "The Biggest Little City in the World!"

Norm Nielson

*AT THE SHORES OF PYRAMID LAKE. This early artist rendering shows the arrival of Capt. John C. Fremont at Pyramid Lake during his first expedition into Nevada in 1843. "We camped opposite a very large rock which had attracted our attention for many miles . . . (it) presented an exact outline of the great pyramid of Cheops." Photo courtesy of the Nevada Historical Society*

# The Beginning

When you compare Reno, Nevada, to towns of the East, she's a pup indeed. At a time when sophisticated columnists were bitterly complaining that such cities as New York and Philadelphia were already bursting at the seams, Reno, Nevada, was still nameless—no more than a stopping-off place on the way to somewhere else.

The earliest visitors never gave the area a second thought. It was merely a sprawling meadow. Nonetheless, the soggy marshland provided a welcome respite after the travails of the Great Plains. It was a place to rest before tackling the one remaining barrier to the "Promised Land" of California: the Sierra Nevada.

Trapper Jedediah Smith was the first white man generally credited with showing more than a passing interest in the region. The year was 1825. Until that time there was not a single American who was remotely aware of this part of the country. To most Easterners, the West was distant, obscure, inhabited by wild beasts and savages. The handful of grizzled explorers that had crossed the Mississippi had carefully avoided any desert regions, following, instead, the large and relatively safe inland rivers to the north.

But men like Smith, and others that followed, were a breed unto themselves. Most had come West not out of chance, despair, or even fear, but by choice. In the same manner as men had charted the oceans before them, these buckskin-clad, so-called "mountainmen" disappeared into the vast and forbidding, yet beautiful, wilderness for literally years at a time. Unlike those who came after them, they were not seeking fabulous wealth. They sought instead a solitude. A $500 annual hoard of beaver, fox, bear, and wolf was more wealth than any had ever seen. It was sufficient; no, it was a more than sufficient reason to endure the incredible hardship.

Smith was bent on discovering a direct route to the Pacific Ocean. For years Indian legend had told of a mighty river that flowed from high in the Rockies all the way to the Pacific coast. If such a river actually existed....

The trail he followed brought his party through what is now western Wyoming. He camped along the shores of a new tributary which he promptly named "Mary's River,"
after his Indian wife who had accompanied him as interpreter.

From the banks of the Mary, Smith turned southwest. After several attempts to locate a notch at the crest of the Sierra, he finally made it to the top and then down into what is now known as northern California. Finding the area warm and to his liking, he left the majority of his party to winter there. Smith and two others began the return trip, this time taking a different route.

They soon came upon a body of water which they called the Dead Sea (the modern-day Mono Lake). There, while exploring along its shores, they came across small nuggets of gold at the water's edge which had been exposed by the tides and the torrential spring rains. They spent several days accumulating nuggets before continuing their journey home. The find left Smith convinced that even the desert had a lot to offer.

So successful was his initial expedition that upon his return to camp along the Green River, Smith, with the help of some of his Dead Sea color (gold), was able to form his own outfit—aptly named the Rocky Mountain Fur Company. He outfitted another expedition immediately.

But his second sojourn met with disaster. This time, as he headed south toward the Colorado River, the party was confronted by hostile Indians. After a pitched battle that lasted a day and a half, only Smith and two others of a party that had initially numbered more than two dozen were still alive. Under cover of darkness, without food or water, they made good their escape and found their way again into the relative safety of Old California.

But there, instead of being welcomed after their ordeal, they were promptly arrested by Mexican authorities. The Mexican government, fearful of the increasing numbers of Americans who just happened to "stumble" into their territory, and convinced that the American government was clandestinely preparing to mount an invasion from the east, threw them into a stockade. Only when Smith managed to produce a document in which the United States superintendent of Indian Affairs had given him written permission to trade with the Indians, was he freed. The expedition left immediately for Great Salt Lake.

Still, the mystique of the new land continued to draw

others. Milton Sublette, another partner in the Rocky Mountain Fur Company, set out in early 1832 to retrace Smith's steps.

This time it was not hostiles, but famine, that struck. The winter had been unusually harsh and Sublette and his men found little game to sustain them. Within a few short weeks, their supplies had been depleted. The men were forced to survive on what few beaver they managed to trap along the way. Unbeknownst to them, the beaver had been having a difficult winter as well. As their own food supply began to dwindle, the beaver had begun to feed off the shoots of wild parsnips that grew in abundance in the area. The flesh of the beaver suddenly became poisonous. Within hours most of the men became violently ill, too ill to travel.

Weakened by the ordeal, the expedition placed several men on travois and turned north in search of food. They found little, and were forced to live off ground crickets and ants. When these insects disappeared, they took to chewing on their own moccasins, then to drinking a pudding made from the blood of their pack animals.

Although Sublette's attempt to map the area had turned into disaster, most of the men managed to survive. It would be another decade, however, before another serious attempt to map the desert wilderness would be made.

In 1843, Capt. John Fremont picked up the gauntlet of discovery. Fremont was still convinced of the existence of a gigantic river which would link the Rockies with San Francisco Bay, and, unlike Smith and Sublette, he would be blessed with more than sufficient men, weapons, and supplies. With funding from the United States government and with much fanfare and flag waving, Fremont set out to conduct the first official charting of the region. (Some modern historians contend that Fremont was not on a simple mapping expedition. Rather, said some members of Congress, he had been secretly enlisted by none other than the president of the United States to scout the most direct overland route into Alta California to pave the way for an invasion onto Mexican soil. While it is true that the American president was considering an attempt to undermine the dominance of Mexico in the region, the importance of the Fremont Expedition in this scheme of national expansion was never proven.)

The meticulous diaries of John Fremont were the first true glimpses of what would eventually become known as Nevada. Newspapers carried excerpts of his journey, and Americans longing for news from the "great American West" were enthralled.

Fremont's first entry conveyed both his excitement and fear. "A great part of it," he wrote, "is absolutely new to geographical, botanical and geological science. We were evidently on the verge of the desert which had been reported to us. The appearance of the country is so forbidding that I was afraid to enter it." But enter he did, and some of Nevada's most famous landmarks shortly were discovered.

When the party first came upon the desert, rather than head directly south through the desolate expanse, Fremont wisely chose to hug the eastern slope of the Sierra Nevada. Within two weeks, the expedition came upon a hidden lake which seemed to rise mysteriously from the desert floor.

"It is a sheet of pure green water, some 20 miles broad," described Fremont. "It broke upon our eyes like an ocean. We camped on the shore opposite a very remarkable rock which had attracted our attention for many miles. It rose, according to our estimate, about 600 feet from the water, presenting an exact outline of the great Pyramid of Cheops. The striking feature suggested a name for the lake and I called it Pyramid." (Fremont's description was accurate. One hundred and twenty years later Hollywood producers, looking for the modern-day equivalent of the Sea of Galilee, chose Pyramid Lake as a location for the movie *The Bible*. The smooth green expanse and the austere surroundings were a perfect match for the terrain of the ancient cradle of civilization.)

Around every bend, over every gentle rise, a strange new world opened to Fremont and his men. As a reward, each new landmark was given the name of one of the expeditioners—the Carson River for scout Christopher "Kit" Carson, the Walker River and Walker Lake for John Walker. The body of water that had been named Mary's River by Jed Smith more than two decades before was renamed the Humboldt after another in the party. On reaching the crest of the Sierra, Fremont named a huge blue body of water Lake Bonpland, in honor of French botanist Amade Bonpland. (To this day, however, people still prefer the original Indian name, *Tahoe*.)

Fremont was careful to avoid confrontations with the local Indians whenever possible. His directive from the government had warned against antagonizing the "aboriginies" and, for the most part, he complied. He even employed the services of one of the locals, a minor chieftain known as Truckee, to guide him along a portion of his route. So helpful was the Indian that Fremont bestowed his own rank, that of honorary captain, upon him. (Whether Truckee was a true Indian name, or merely another case of phonetic mispronunciation, is still not known. Early accounts agree that the Truckee River which winds its way down to the valley floor from Lake Tahoe was named for the Indian. Whether the name was bestowed by Fremont or by a later party headed by Captain Stevens is still a matter of speculation.)

Without locating the elusive river he had sought, Fremont, like Smith and Sublette before him, continued his journey into Alta California. Here he rested his men and animals for three months while enjoying little confrontation with Mexican authorities.

On his return, he had considerably more confidence and more respect for the region. In the summer of 1844 he wrote, "It is such a fascinating land. For all its hardship, I shall hate to leave it!"

Whether he was an extraordinary explorer or merely a government spy in the employ of the president, Fremont, nonetheless, would parlay his travels into a career that would make him both wealthy and famous. Soon the Eastern press had dubbed him "the pathfinder," and he would go on to make an unsuccessful bid for the presidency within a few years.

But his role in the far West was considerably more important because Fremont had for the first time truly opened the door to Western expansion. When news of his expedition swept the Eastern Seaboard, thousands of settlers hungry for free land and a new adventure would

*THE DONNER PARTY
REMEMBERED. This poignant statue,
erected in front of the State Building in the
early 1950s, today stands in the plaza of
Reno's Pioneer Center for the Performing
Arts. Although the Donner party met a
tragic fate, stories of which swept the nation,
the disaster did little to stem the tide of
western movement. Photo courtesy of
Neal Cobb*

follow in his footsteps. (Fremont's meticulous maps were printed as well.) By the next year, wagon trains began to push west and the rush of humanity was on. An Independence, Missouri, man, Edwin Bryant wrote a book entitled *What I Saw In California.* He described the migration through the Nevada portion of the territory in 1846: "The number of emigrants on the road I estimate to be 3,000. I have met, by last count, 430 wagons along the way."

Not all of the emigrant trains would be successful. It was early in the fall when the ill-fated Donner party reached what was becoming known as the Truckee Meadows. They had spent more than four months on the trail and the group had split, some preferring to head north into Oregon, a route much safer and more familiar at the time.

Having already endured the usual hardships of most wagon trains—death from old age, tongues burning and thickened with thirst, skins blackened by the scorching heat—it was no wonder that when they had finally reached the foot of the Sierra Nevada they were convinced that the worst was over.

On October 20, 1846, the group faced a major decision. Brave the Sierra or stay, that was the question. Press on immediately (for other travelers had patiently assured them that winter was still weeks away) or spend another four or five months just a scant one hundred and twenty miles from journey's end. They decided to go on.

Just a few days from the safety of the Meadows, the snow began to fall. Daily, endlessly it fell, the depth soon increasing not by inches but by feet. Near what would later become known as Donner Lake, travel in the blinding snows was no longer possible. The snow had piled to a depth of more than thirty feet. Trees were obscured by the blinding whiteness. The party decided to camp, to wait it out in winter silence. The numbing cold permeated, said one survivor, "the very soul."

As supplies slowly dwindled, what little remained was doled out in painstaking fashion. Oxen were killed for food. Some members of the group had gone on ahead. Though they managed to reach the safety of the California foothills, it would be agonizing weeks before the fury of the storm abated enough to allow them to attempt a rescue mission.

By then it was too late. Upon returning to the campsite, they found the cabins buried beneath drifts four times the height of a normal man. Many within the party had perished. Of those still alive, men were now too exhausted to stand, women too weak to cry. But there was something else. There were bones, human bones, all that remained of men and women who had once been friends, hopeful companions on the road to the promised land. In the months that followed, lurid tales of cannibalism flashed across the nation, but not even the horror of the Donner party's fate would slow the now-endless westward river of humanity.

It would be two more years before the last great obstacle to American domination of the West would tumble. A war with Mexico soon broke out and on February 2, 1848, the Mexican government signed a treaty with the victorious Americans, backdated it to 1846, and Alta California officially became a part of the United States. Under the terms of the agreement, all of the Mexican territory between the Pacific Ocean and the Rocky Mountains came under the domain of the United States. It encompassed an expanse which was bordered on the north by the present-day California-Oregon line and on the south by the winding Gila River.

The treaty had an even greater effect on the residents who lived in the shadow of the Sierra. It deeded a huge amount of territory which soon became the states of Arizona, New Mexico, and Nevada.

The die was cast. Adding to the excitement was the fact that soon there would be an interesting discovery at an obscure place called Sutter's Mill.

*THE FIRST TRUE SETTLERS. This old Mormon fort and trading post was built in 1851 by James and Enoch Reese. Located in Mormon Station (later Genoa), it was one of the first permanent structures in Nevada. Photo courtesy of the Nevada Historical Society*

# The Settlers

*Alkalai plains, covered in part with scattering sage
brush; basaltic rocks twisted and contorted with great
convulsions of Nature over which the lizard darts in
his daily hunt for a dinner of insects. How the
horned toad, crickets, rabbits and sage hen manage
to survive passes the understanding of the average
ox-driver who wends his toilsome way towards the
setting sun. What such a country was made for—so
useless, so God-forsaken, was the standing question
always entering into consideration, whether watch-
ing the cattle during the long hours of the night or
forcing them onward with the lash during the day.
To the average emigrant, the land is repulsive in
the extreme.*

*Unknown Pioneer, circa 1850*

And perhaps it was.
Even as late as 1859, when the word of Nevada's
riches had finally circled the globe, editor Horace
Greeley wrote disparagingly, "It would be better for us all
if the Sierra Nevada and the Rocky Mountains could be
brought together and all the country in between could be
eliminated from the surface of the earth."

Still, in the mid-1840s, few seemed to notice.
Americans by the thousands were making their way West
in search of soil "as rich as Eden"—those words would
take on a new meaning by 1849.

When news of the fabulous gold strike at Sutter's Mill
in California flashed across the country, a new breed of
Americans was suddenly on the move. Prior to the discovery of gold, most emigrants braving the trail were looking
for farmland; now there was a rush only to riches. In a
hectic attempt to be the first upon the scene, men without
the slightest knowledge of what lay ahead deserted their
families and headed West. Before, it was the family unit
that had sought to populate the area; now single men
converged on the West, and not a few were a step ahead of
the law. Mixed into the throng with righteous, God-fearing
families were card sharks, convicts, and confidence men.

Constant name changes made law enforcement difficult.

The years between 1849 and 1852 were fabulous
indeed. Newspaper headlines trumpeted that nuggets "as
big as a fist" were just sticking right up out of the ground.
The popular phrase Promised Land took on new meaning
as men from all walks of life flooded into the California
foothills in search of instant wealth.

There were riches there, of course, incredible
discoveries that would boggle even the most active,
imaginative mind. But, as so often is the case, most of it
was snapped up by those first upon the scene. By the time
the majority of gold seekers had reached what many were
calling the Mother Lode, they found the diggings hopelessly
played out and prices for such essentials as beans, flour,
and lard exorbitant for even the best prepared.

All of this would matter little to the majority of those
who chose to settle in Nevada at this time; for the first true
settlers were searching not for wealth, but for freedom
from religious persecution.

The Mormons had braved a tumultuous mass journey
west (the hardships of which would rival the trials of even
the most seasoned pioneers). Forced from their homes in
the Northeast by religious leaders who were horrified by

the belief that a golden angel had appeared to spiritual leader Joseph Smith, the Mormon faithful had been driven relentlessly west—eventually forming a permanent city on the banks of the Great Salt Lake. Determined never again to suffer such degradation, Mormon leader Brigham Young had ordered his followers to expand even further—across much of the area of what is now Nevada. The directive: to establish trade routes and create new settlements.

On March 18, 1849, Mormon elders assembled at a convention and organized a "territorial government." That government, it was determined, would preside over what was to be called the State of Deseret.

The State was an ambitious undertaking. It was to consist of all the land which today encompasses Utah, Nevada, Arizona, and parts of present-day Colorado, Oregon, and Wyoming. Even a part of southern California was included (portions of choice land which today are Los Angeles and San Diego counties in the south and Santa Monica in the north).

The United States government, however, didn't take too kindly to the idea of a separate state created by a religious entity. There had been an ongoing confrontation between Mormon leaders and the government for years. In Washington, congressmen railed against the sophisticated, though sometimes far-fetched, attempts to take over what amounted to almost one-quarter of the American continent.

Six months later, on September 9, the very day on which California was admitted to the Union, Congress created a state of its own. They called it the Utah Territory and it stretched from California east to the Rockies, north to Oregon, and south to the Thirty-seventh Parallel.

But the Mormon elders took little notice. They systematically continued their efforts to colonize the region. Spreading out, along dry creek beds that would soon become wagon trails, they established settlements in the south, such as the fort which would eventually become the thriving mission in Las Vegas. In the north, the Mormon elders created Nevada's first true community, Mormon Station (later Genoa), on the southern end of sprawling Carson Valley. So successful were church pioneers, that they succeeded in acquiring the first government contract to carry the United States mail.

Mormon farms began to dot the northern portion of the territory with incredible frequency. While hungry gold-seekers were practically trampling each other in the race to the gold fields, hearty and dedicated Mormon farmers were laying claim to the land along the way.

One early settler, Robert Lyon, described Mormon Station as he remembered it when passing through in 1850:

I arrived at the Station and lay resting for one day. I sold a good American horse to the man who kept the trading post for 30 pounds of flour and $15.00. Flour was $1.50 a pound so he allowed me $60.00 for my horse. There were two or three women at the place and I understood that they had settled there with the impression of remaining permanently. They had quite a band of cattle they had brought over from Salt Lake;

some of the fattest cows I have ever seen hung suspended from the limbs of a big pine tree. They retailed the beef to hungry emigrants for 75 cents a pound. I have never since eaten beef that tasted so sweet.

In regard to improvements, there was one store where they kept for sale flour, beans, tea, coffee, sugars, shirts, etc., and there was also a grocery where they sold whiskey, bread, cigars and tobacco. There was one good sized house under construction but I was told it was intended for a family dwelling and meeting house. As you see, Mormon Station was well established. . . .

Mormon expansion continued. On December 1, 1852, the first land claim was filed in the region. John Reese applied for a tract of land which stretched from the fledgling Mormon Station to the base of the Sierra and to the Carson River. In partnership with Israel Mott, Reese applied for a franchise to place a toll bridge across the Carson. They placed $1,000 on deposit for upkeep of the bridge and began making money the very first day. Wagons were charged one dollar, horned cattle ten cents. Sheep could cross for two and a half cents, and mules were charged a quarter. It became the first true business in the territory.

But the Mormon settlement would be short-lived. In 1856 a group of Mormons had driven a Utah federal judge from his bench at gunpoint. Enraged, President James Buchanan sent a small army under the command of General Sidney Johnston to restore order and the supremacy of the United States government in the region. Learning that government troops were on the march, Brigham Young sent word to the faithful to pull up stakes immediately and return to defend Salt Lake City.

On September 5, a dispatch arrived in the valley and hurriedly area Mormons packed up their belongings for the trip. By September 26, more than four hundred and fifty people had assembled in one hundred and twenty three wagons filled to overflowing with whatever worldly possessions they managed to collect. Title to property was simply abandoned or transferred at a pittance to adjacent Gentiles. Within hours, other wagon trains from Oregon and California began to arrive and together they departed.

The hasty exodus left the Truckee, Washoe, Carson, and adjacent valleys almost deserted as the Mormon population retreated to defend against a military confrontation that would never materialize. Still, feelings ran high. On January 27, 1863, Mormon pioneer Orson Hyde, who had tried unsuccessfully for years to receive some compensation for a sawmill he had abandoned, wrote an open letter to the people of Carson Valley:

You shall be visited by the Lord of hosts with thunder and with earthquakes and with floods. You shall be visited with pestilence and famine until your names are not known amongst men for you have rejected the authority of God, trampled upon His laws and His ordinances. You have given yourself up to debauchery, abominations, drunkenness and corruption. If there is an honest man among you I would advise him to leave, but let him not go to California for safety for he will not find it there.

But not everyone left.

On August 3, 1857, a gathering was held in Gilbert's Saloon in Mormon Station to plead for some form of government. It was the first public meeting ever held in the region, and a popular jurist, Judge Crane, was elected to represent the settlers of the valley in Congress.

The group drafted a resolution that stated:

Whereas, the people inhabiting the territory commonly known as the Great American Basin, lying between the eastern spurs and foothills of the Sierra Nevada, west of the Goose Creek range of mountains and the Oregon line on the north and the Colorado and its tributaries on the south—having become convinced from the rapid expansion in population within these limits, the dangers which threaten us from the numerous tribes of Indians and from the absence of law to restrain the vicious and protect the upright, that some kind of government should be established as soon as possible for the better security of life and property.

Resolved, that for the better security of their life and property, as well as those of the emigrants crossing the continent, a Territorial Government should be organized by Congress within the shortest period of time.

An open letter to the President was drafted:

The citizens inhabiting the valleys within the Great Basin of the American Continent beg leave respectfully to present for the consideration of the President of the United States and both houses of Congress their petition praying for the organization of a new Territory of the United States. We do not propose to come with any flourish of trumpets but to simply submit a few plain statements as inducements to those who have the power to remedy the difficulties and embarrassments under which we now labor and suffer.

A large portion of the inhabitants making this appeal to the powers that be in Washington have been in the region for the past 6 or 7 years without any Territorial, State, or Federal protection from Indian depredations and marauding outlaws, runaway criminals and convicts as well as evil doers.

The appeal continued for page after page, and even included a map showing the isolation of the valleys, particularly during winter months. They pleaded, they cajoled, they evoked the wisdom of God—all to no avail. It would still be years before Congress would be convinced. And perhaps for good reason.

Unlike native Americans in much of the country,

Nevada's Indians were far from hostile. Indeed, for decades they had been extremely helpful to the white population (from Chief Truckee right on down). An article which was printed in the *Sacramento State Journal* dated 1857 stated:

The Indians are broken up into many bands. The Paiutes are much the largest in number, being about 40,000. They are not hostile to Americans and have never favored the Mormons. They are friendly toward the new territory and indeed anxious for it. They desire to cultivate the arts of peace and become tillers of the soil.

They are the best servants in America and have shown themselves to be excellent cooks, farmers, herdsmen and mechanics. All the other tribes are war-like, insincere, treacherous and blood thirsty. Should the Territory be organized, the Paiutes would promptly unite with the whites and identify themselves with the peaceful progress of the country.

Meanwhile in the region that would eventually become known as Reno, early pioneers were finding a welcome haven after the travails of the desert. Vincent Geiger, who entered the Steamboat Springs area in 1849, was jubilant. "We have crossed a slough," he wrote, "the crossing of which was fixed and bridged by our captain and the party ahead. Before this was done, it is said it was almost impassable, each [wagon] having to be cordelled across. We passed over it safely and encamped in this lovely valley, with blue grass to the horses knees."

That same year, Elisha Perkins arrived in the Truckee Meadows. Perkins took a route that brought his party near the site of the present-day Hidden Valley Country Club, and from there they turned west beneath the shadow of Rattlesnake Mountain. He described it as follows:

At 4 p.m., we emerged from the canyon into what is called Mist Valley, a beautiful level plain covered with fine grass, some 10 miles across and formed by the widening of the mountain ranges. Through this valley the river winds after leaving the gorge from the other side, its course marked by a line of willows and cottonwoods. Soon after entering the valley we took a trail leaving the road to the right and wound around a belt of marsh which crosses the valley at right angles to the river....

The view from our present camp is grand. In front of us towers a range of the loftiest mountains we have yet seen, their tops covered with perpetual snow....

The Truckee Meadows had then become a place to rest for those headed relentlessly west.

By 1852 most of the dreams of instant wealth in California had faded. Miners, reluctant to return to their homes empty handed, began to look elsewhere. Some, pick in hand, deliberately headed back over the Sierra retracing steps they had trodden but a few short months before. Some decided to try their luck en route, to prospect a bit

*THEY NEVER STRUCK IT RICH.*
*This early rendering (circa 1850) shows the*
*Grosch brothers, Hosea and Ethan Allen.*
*They were the first to uncover the rich*
*silver deposits in the desolate shadow of*
*Sun Mountain, but both died tragically*
*before they could reap the benefits of their*
*discovery. Photo courtesy of the Nevada*
*Historical Society*

"over Nevada way" before returning East to their meager farms.

That year, the Grosch brothers, Hosea and Ethan Allen, were working the diggings near Johnstown (later Dayton). They were well educated as prospectors went, the sons of a Universalist clergyman, A. B. Grosch, who had been the editor of a religious newspaper in Utica, New York. Unlike most of the gold seekers, the brothers had actually studied metallurgy before coming west.

But in the summer of 1852, the Groschs were alternating equally between back-breaking labor and starvation. For weeks, they would move slowly, painstakingly, up the slopes of a mountain (which would later become known as Mount Davidson); then, in desperation, they would return to California to work at other tasks in order to assemble another grubstake. Armed with fresh supplies, they would return again to the place known as Gold Canyon.

The giant arroyo was living up to its name, though sparingly. For several years, miners had been finding color (gold) in the sagebrush-strewn, arid landscape, and the "big bonanza" was out there someplace—they were sure of it.

They were a motley crew, those gaunt, wizened men of the Canyon. In addition to the young brothers, there was a teamster (often called lazy by his friends), James Fennimore, also known as James Finney, and two Irishmen, Peter O'Riley and Patrick McLaughlin. Perhaps the strangest of the breed was a gregarious fellow by the name of Henry Comstock—"Old Pancake" they called him, for his affinity for flapjacks.

It has been said that mining camps are like tin cans, they spring up where they lie, and along the slopes of Mount Davidson it was certainly true, as the notes of John Bishop attest:

> I had noticed indication of a ledge and had got a little color. I asked Ol' Virginny (James Finney) about it and he said he remembered the locality from hunting deer and antelope there. I began washing my pan and when I finished I found that I had about 15 cents. None of the others had less than 8 cents and some had 15. It was very fine gold.
>
> After we had measured the ground we had a consultation as to what name was to be given the place. It was decidedly not Gold Canyon. It was just a little hill so we concluded to call it that.

While the camp began to take root, further up the slope, others were experiencing some luck of their own. Emanuel Penrod, who was there at the time, later recalled in a letter from Elko:

Peter O'Riley and Patrick McLaughlin were prospecting at what is now the Ophir Mine when ol' Virginny came along and said 'Boys, you've struck it!'

Now Henry Comstock and myself owned nine of the ten shares of the spring that furnished water for working the mine. So we were asked to buy up the other shares in the area. I got a bill of sale from Finney, White and Curby for the whole of the ground and I paid $50.00 for it, I think. Comstock gave an old blind horse for his share of the water.

Unbeknownst to Penrod and the others, that claim lay atop what would eventually be termed the Comstock Lode.

While most of the men were bent on discovering that elusive outcropping of gold-bearing quartz which, as in California, would be "sticking right up out of the ground," the Groschs were convinced that the ore in the area lay deeper; not on the surface, as most supposed, but underground. Additionally, they were not totally convinced that all that glittered was gold at all.

For months, many of the prospectors had been confounded by a substance that they referred to as "that infernal blue stuff." It stuck to picks and shovels, frustrating earth-moving efforts. It was an excruciating chore to move the "blue stuff" out of the way. They cursed the strange substance as they carelessly heaved it down the mountainside.

But the Grosch brothers, with their metallurgical background, knew better. They had a hunch that the "blue stuff" was sulpheret of silver and were convinced they were on to something. In September of 1856, after coming across two gigantic veins, they were positive. Excitedly, they wrote home—"We have discovered the perfect monsters!" Armed with samples, they journeyed again over the Sierra to the closest assayer.

Amazingly enough, the sample proved almost worthless, yet the brothers would not give up. They made the rounds again trying to scrounge up enough backing to mount a full-scale assault on their find, but they were thwarted at every turn. "Quartz mining is just too risky. It requires too much equipment. Too expensive," came the reply. Discouraged, the brothers returned once again to the canyon.

But this time while they were working their claim, something extraordinary was happening in another part of the region. A Carson City rancher, by the name of Morrison, happened by the diggings and, being curious, pocketed some of the "blue stuff" that most of the miners had been throwing carelessly aside. On his next trip to California he stopped by the Grass Valley assay office of J. J. Ott, who confirmed what Morrison had only suspected. The "stuff" contained $1,595 in gold but more important, $3,196 in silver! The ore assayed out at an incredible $4,790 a ton.

Comstock reporter William Wright, who would win notoriety under the pen name of Dan DeQuille, picks up the story from there. "The excitement was by no means abated when the men of Grass Valley were informed by Mr. Morrison that there were tons and tons of the stuff in plain sight right at the opening to the Ophir and it was wisely agreed that the matter should be kept a profound secret."

It would prove to be impossible. Within hours, men were packed and ready to set out across the mountains. Wrote Wright: "By nine o'clock the next morning, half the town of Grass Valley had heard the wonderful news. In a few days hundreds of miners had left their diggings in California and were flocking over the mountains on horseback, on foot, with teams and in any way that offered." While the unwitting brothers, now close to starvation, continued to scour the canyon, throughout northern California the word was spreading—"On to Washoe!" was the cry.

Unaware of the second assay, the Groschs were still working their claim when disaster struck. Hosea pierced his foot with a pick. Blood poisoning soon set in. Within days he died in their bleak stone cabin at the entrance to American Flat Ravine.

After burying his brother, the tenacious Allen Grosch set out once again for California. Armed with additional samples, he was confident they would prove the real value of his ore.

It was November when Grosch and a companion, Richard Burke, began. But this time it would be Mother Nature who stepped in. At the summit, a blizzard caught up with them. After weeks of wallowing in chest-deep whiteness, blinded by driving snow, their food supply ran out. At night, they burrowed deep into the drifts for warmth. Like the Donner party before them, they slaughtered their donkey and ate it. Suddenly, the storm ended.

Within a few days, the men stumbled into a mining camp on the western slope. But while he rested, Allen Grosch would hear the rumors, the stories of the fabulous strike up in the Nevadas, of a silver find so pure that it was beyond imagination. Grosch began to realize that the strike of which they spoke was his.

His elation soon turned to horror. His feet had been frozen in the raging blizzard and frostbite had set in. Within another week Allen Grosch, heir to one of the greatest fortunes in the country's history, was dead.

But a new era was beginning.

*VIRGINIA CITY—THE MOST RAUCOUS BOOMTOWN IN THE WEST. It sprang up almost overnight, dangling precariously on the mountainside. Though known as a "metropolitan city" with some of the finest hotels in the West, it was also known for its violence. Wrote actor/producer David Belasco, "I was one of the first to bring naturalness to my death scenes. My experiences in Virginia City did much to help me toward this." Photo courtesy of the Nevada Historical Society*

# The Miners

By the fall of 1860, the rush to Washoe had escalated. It was now a full-scale torrent of rough-hewn humanity, and the going was rough. Most of the men refused to wait for the coming of spring. Instead, they loaded whatever pack animals that could be had and struck out blindly into the snow. After a few miles, the animals bogged down and the men, now helpless in the endless drifts, took to spreading blankets out in front of them as they moved inches at a time across the crusted whiteness. Soon they were stranded. An emergency load of supplies, ordered by Nevada's newly appointed acting Territorial Governor Kinkead, arrived, having traveled mile after tortuous mile in the same blanketing fashion.

"They came on foot, driving donkeys or on horseback when they could," wrote Comstock reporter DeQuille in his diary. "Soon sleighs and stages were started and they floundered with their passengers. Saddle trains were started but in some places the snow ranged from 30 to 60 feet in depth. At first there was little shelter for the newcomers and they crowded to overflowing every shelter of whatever kind along the Comstock range."

Wrote an unknown prospector on April 5, 1860: "Ever since I have been here the wind has been blowing continuously day and night with double the intensity of the afternoon winds which prevail most of the year on Telegraph Hill and North Beach in San Francisco. I'm told these winds prevail here nearly ¾'s of the year."

The miners, used to the balmy California climate, were in for a frightening surprise. Alf Doten, reminiscing in his elaborate diary of the Comstock, wrote in 1881: "They lived in tents and brush houses covered with dirt. They burrowed into rocks and tunnels by twos, half dozens or as many as 20 men at a time. It was one of the most dreary, comfortless, severely cold winters ever known in Nevada, and the men were warmed by scant wood and cheered only by a golden hope in the future." Wrote one prospector: "Snow has been falling for the past 15 hours and there is about one foot of snow on the ground. All business out of doors is stopped."

The snow kept falling. More than five feet was noted in a single twenty-four hour period. Reporter DeQuille would later observe, "The stomachs of many had frequent holidays."

Perhaps it was nature's warning to those stampeding recklessly toward Nevada. That first winter, the wind would whistle along at fifty miles an hour and the snow would drift to more than eight feet along the slopes of the silver mountain.

Surprisingly enough, the area that was attracting the most attention was still without a name. Men were calling the region the Comstock, for it was Old Pancake who bragged to newcomers that he had been first on the scene. Popular folklore contends that James Finney, a native of Virginia, had, in a drunken stupor, slipped and spilled a bottle of his favorite libation. Rising to his feet, he proclaimed, "I christen this spot Virginny!" The story of Virginia City's beginning has persisted to this day.

Regardless, there was little evidence that the daily torrent of arrivals would soon create one of the largest cities west of the Mississippi. Dr. Pierson recalled the scene in a letter to the *Carson Tribune*:

I visited the spot known as Virginia and found not a house, but two tents on the ground, one owned by John L. Blackburn who later died of an assassin's knife. I saw the mine and formed an acquaintance with Mr. Comstock, the man whose name is perpetuated wherever mines are known throughout the world. Also old gentleman Virginia for whom the place is named. On that day in June the writer saw $1900 in black gold (value $11 an ounce) washed out of the surface ground at the Ophir.

The frenzy continued. In the haste to stake a claim, any claim, record keeping was almost non-existent and few people seemed to care. The region's first recorder, V. A. Houseworth, a part-time blacksmith, kept his record book at a wood and canvas saloon, in plain sight behind the bar. In it were such scribbled entries as "Notice. We the undersigned, claim 600 feet of this quartz vein, commencing with the south end of Finney and Co. and running south 600 feet and two chains." It was signed Peter O'Riley and Patrick McLaughlin, the two men generally credited as the true discoverers of the Comstock Lode.

Other claims were unfortunately not as specific. One began, "We, the undersigned, claim 2,000 feet of this quartz land, ledge, lode, or vein, beginning at the end of the stake and running north." There was absolutely no mention of where the aforementioned stake could be found.

Since Houseworth's book was open for all to see, one simply asked the bartender for a look-see. Naturally, this led to changes that were not altogether above-board. Pages were indiscriminately torn from the ledger; dates and descriptions were simply crossed out and written in again.

Just the same, many finds were yielding riches which to this day are unequaled in America. Comstock and Company, yielding two common gold rockers, was averaging more than $500 a day per rocker. Bishop and Company was bringing in about $205, and William Knight, a reporter notes, was pulling down $400 daily.

But while the Comstock Lode was bracing itself for assault, the rest of the territory was still desolate. During the winter of 1859, three feet of snow covered the Ruby Valley to the northeast and livestock perished by the hundreds.

In Humboldt County, J. P. Waters, a United States deputy marshal reported, "There are no inhabitants in the region at all, save those who are charged with the mail service. The only things not human seen living are snakes, lizards and crickets, upon which the local Indians are forced to feed for a portion of the year."

The rush to Virginia City continued. As the men clamored recklessly for instant wealth, an event was taking place further to the east, an event that would signal the end of peace in the territory. Truckee, the man who had befriended early whites and had guided John Fremont on his initial expedition, was dying.

In 1860, as old age began to overtake the Paiute leader, he was bitten on the cheek by a tarantula and almost immediately lapsed into a coma. Word spread throughout the region that the old man was dying and signal fires burned from mountaintops as members of the tribe began to gather.

Miraculously, Truckee regained consciousness and called his family to him. He urged a continuation of peace with the whites who now were approaching in ever-increasing numbers, killing game with wild abandon, and destroying the pine nut trees (a centuries-old Indian staple for food and firewood).

The chieftain had left specific instructions regarding his burial. He wanted a white man's cross erected and his body laid to rest in a particular fashion, with his arms crossed upon his chest. A medal given to him by Fremont was to be buried with him.

When he finally succumbed to death, family members were stymied as to the strange burial procedures. Some whites who were passing through were brought to the grave site to assist. Once the body had been lowered, six of the chief's best horses were slaughtered Indian-fashion and a eulogy was given by his son-in-law, Captain John. John's poignant speech, as recorded in *History of Nevada 1881*, states:

*THE FLEDGLING REPORTER. In early October 1862, a broke and discouraged Sam Clemens arrived in Virginia City to take a job at the* Territorial Enterprise. *It was while serving his apprenticeship that he would adopt his pen name, Mark Twain. Photo courtesy of the Nevada Historical Society*

A good man is gone. The white man knows he was good for he guided him around deserts and led him in paths where there was grass and good water. His people knew he was good for he loved them and cared for them and came home to them to die. All know that Truckee was a good man— Paiutes and Americans. He is dead; the good man is gone. All people cry, for they loved Truckee.

With Truckee gone, most whites feared that the peace they had enjoyed for so long would end. Sadly, they were right. Within a matter of months there would be a massacre along the river that bore his name, and the Indian uprising (which became known as the Pyramid Lake Indian War) would take place.

But most whites were too busy to care. Although the miners along the Comstock went armed and even erected a barricade complete with an ominous-looking but useless wooden cannon at the entrance to the lode, most were too

*"THE HEARTIEST WORKERS ALIVE!"* These men endured temperatures of 160 degrees at depths of more than twelve hundred feet below the streets of Virginia City. Shown here are workers from the Ophir (top left), the Savage (bottom left), the Gould and Curry (top right), and the Chollar (bottom right). The men centered are brothers who lost their lives in a fire at the Gold Hill Mine on April 7, 1869. Photo courtesy of the Nevada Historical Society

absorbed in the headlong search for wealth.

For the next twenty years, the Comstock Lode would yield riches unheard of in their magnitude. Names like Mackay, Fair, Flood, and O'Brian emerged. Mines like the Hale and Norcross, the Ophir, the Belcher, the Crown Point, and others became household words. One of the most famous, the Consolidated Virginia and California, would pay out more than $100 million to its shareholders between 1874 and 1879 alone. ·

The work underground was back-breaking, dangerous, and offered little reward. The average wage, though the highest in the industry, was a mere four dollars a day at a time when the cost of a room, if indeed one could be found, was usually twenty dollars a week.

Below ground, at the twelve-hundred-foot level, temperatures reached an unbelievable 130 degrees. Men could only work for a few hours at a time, then were forced to retreat to rest areas where they chewed ice to cool themselves down. It is estimated that almost 10 percent of

the men who worked below ground during the heyday of the Comstock were either killed or maimed.

In their haste to tunnel ever deeper into the belly of the earth, the miners stripped the surrounding terrain of trees. Tunnels required lumber, and one mine, again the Consolidated, buried lumber at the unheard of rate of six million board feet per year. What wood was unsuitable for shoring was burned as firewood at an estimated rate of more than two hundred and fifty thousand cords annually.

The appetite of the miners was voracious as well. Livestock were driven over the Sierra by the thousands, only to perish in the valleys below for lack of adequate grazing. In a letter to the *Mountain Democrat*, a resident wrote, "Horses and cows are very poor and thousands are seen lying dead all over the valley. They have evidently died of starvation."

Hogs, being hereditary scavengers, however, fared considerably better. Continued the writer, "All the hogs I

*A MARVEL OF ENGINEERING. Adolf Sutro's plan to drill a tunnel more than twenty thousand feet into the bowels of Mount Davidson was spurred on by a series of disastrous fires which trapped many of the workers, burning them alive. His tunnel would go down in history as one of America's finest feats of engineering. Photo courtesy of the Nevada Historical Society*

LEADING THE PARADE. Fire was the most feared enemy on the Comstock. The fact that the earliest fire fighters were volunteer proved to be a vast source of community pride. Many of the town's leading citizens were members. Photo courtesy of the Nevada Historical Society

have seen are in good order, as they have profited much from the carcasses of other animals." He was quick to add, "To think of a fat pork steak under such circumstances is by no means refreshing or consoling to my mind. We have them served up in our restaurants and yet we know not from whence they came."

While excitement raged on Mount Davidson, much of the political power in the region was settling in Carson City. Named for Fremont's guide, the city became the capital of the territory in 1861. Here, far from the squalid living conditions that personified the Comstock, the truly rich were setting up shop. Power began to converge on the city which offered free quarters to the territorial legislature and later, after statehood, to the state government as well.

Trouble was brewing in the east. A civil war was raging and President Abraham Lincoln, hopelessly deadlocked in his attempt to end slavery, cast about for a means to end the conflict. He determined that the only sure way of bringing the issue to rest would be to create an entirely new state. Nevada, rich in wealth, was the obvious choice. Amidst much fanfare, Nevada, a region of isolated ranches and clusters of miners, became a state in 1864. Lincoln had achieved his purpose.

But in Nevada the event was hardly noticed, except by politicians. Wrote reporter Alf Doten in his diary of October 31, 1864, "Clear and pleasant today. At sunrise this morning I was awakened by the bells and steam whistles telling us that there was a fire. I went out and ran to it. It was near the Divide. It was the Golden Eagle Hotel and other buildings.

"Great day for items. I got through at 12 o'clock at night and wrote steadily all evening." Then, as what seems to be an afterthought, Doten concluded, "We got a telegram this morning, announcing that the President has issued a proclamation making us a state. Hurrah for the State of Nevada!"

Meanwhile, Carson City was growing by leaps and bounds. Banks and other symbols of wealth were springing up and tracks for horse-drawn streetcars were laid down.

Its selection as a capital did not come easily. In 1864 a group of Comstock businessmen formed a coalition to bring the seat of government closer to the diggings. On the flat just south of Gold Hill, they laid out an entire town, called American City. They even offered the legislature the princely sum of $50,000 to relocate. The movement gained momentum when Ormsby County, which was suffering temporary financial difficulties, decided to charge the legislature $4,500 annually for the use of their formerly free facilities. Virginia City papers jumped on the bandwagon.

Officials of Ormsby County, realizing their error, circulated a petition criticizing County Commissioner Adolphus Waitz for the situation, and the offer to relocate Nevada's capital city was rejected.

Carson City continued to prosper, and the Comstock Lode continued to disgorge its fabulous wealth. Meanwhile, another town in the new state was beginning to awaken. It was a tiny settlement along the Truckee River. It was called Lake's Crossing.

*THE BRIDGE THAT STARTED IT ALL. This rendering of early Lake's Crossing (circa 1861) shows the first bridge in the region. Myron Lake's toll charges were outrageous even for the time but would make him a wealthy man. Photo courtesy of Reno Orthopedic Clinic*

# The Bridge That Started It All

It was in the spring of 1860 when the first employees of Jones, Russell and Company headed west from St. Joseph, Missouri. Short, wiry youngsters, who were given the somewhat glamorous nickname "Pony Express," they were the first to connect the sleepy little settlement of Lake's Crossing with the rest of the nation on a regular basis, stagecoaches and pack animals being notoriously unreliable at the time.

The year before, a man named Charles Fuller (formerly of Honey Lake, Missouri) had happened upon the Meadows. It was here that the east-west Emigrant Trail crossed the north-south route and a small, but at times turbulent river, the Truckee, had to be traversed.

Fuller knew a good thing when he saw it. He decided to build a bridge across the Truckee and charge people for his trouble. The idea wasn't new, of course. Charles Gates and partner John F. Stone had built a crude toll bridge as early as 1857, but it was washed away by spring flooding. It should have been a warning to Fuller, for that first spring the hapless entrepreneur also met with near disaster. Just when his initial construction was completed, sudden runoff washed away his bridge as well. After several more similar calamities, Fuller had had enough.

Enter Myron Lake, who was much more of an architect than his predecessor. In 1861 he purchased Fuller's property and chose a location slightly further upstream than the place folks had been calling Fuller's Folly. There, using natural stone outcroppings for support, he built another bridge, much stronger this time.

Still, Lake was taking no chances. The wily businessman also laid claim to the roadways for several miles both upstream and down. Should disaster strike again, Lake was fully prepared. Even without a bridge, he could still impose a toll upon travelers moving through the area. He added a tavern (meals could be had for fifty cents) and an inn near the site. His future was virtually assured.

As word of the Comstock silver strikes raced across the country, Myron Lake soon learned that his initial success was merely a drop in the bucket. Truly, he was a man in the right place at the right time. Within just a few short weeks, California miners, prospectors, and assorted hangers-on were bounding across Lake's little toll bridge with a vengeance.

His toll charges were outrageous even for the times. It was fifty cents for a horse and rider and one dollar for a wagon or carriage. Making the situation even more profitable was the fact that the miners of Virginia City were hungry. The only way to get beef to the diggings was on the hoof, across Lake's bridge at the exorbitant fee of one dollar a head.

Lake expanded his operation even further. He constructed a gristmill, a livery, a kiln, and several other outbuildings. In 1862, after passage of the Homestead Act, he added rangeland to the north, east, and west and began raising cattle. His property along the river had, in actuality, become a small but thriving town. By 1861 a telegraph line was constructed from Sacramento to Salt Lake City. It marked the end of the legendary Pony Express, but it was just the beginning for Myron Lake.

The region that bordered the Truckee Meadows was still relatively unsettled. The nearest military outpost was Fort Churchill, established to quell any Indian unrest in the wake of the death of Truckee. The post was so isolated, the conditions so unbearable, that though faced with the very real possibility of being shot by a firing squad as military law allowed, by some estimates 20 percent of the troops stationed there deserted.

None of this bothered Lake. He knew that swiftly on the heels of the transcontinental telegraph would come the railroad. While others scoffed that no one could build a railroad over the treacherous Sierra, Lake remained convinced that political pressure would eventually force its completion, no matter what the odds. He was right.

But despite the tremendous wealth now spewing from the Comstock and the national cry for further western expansion notwithstanding, the rails were slow in coming. First hampered by the financial drain of the Civil War, then by the combined barriers of element and terrain, it would not be until December 13, 1867, that Lake's dream would come true. On that date the first locomotive reached the valley floor.

It would be almost six months later, on May 4, 1868,

before the rails finally reached Lake's Crossing. By then, Lake had formed an ingenious and intimate relationship with Charles Crocker of the Central Pacific Railroad. Crocker, who, along with Leland Stanford, Mark Hopkins, and Collis Huntington, had managed to raise funds for the western portion of the Transcontinental Railroad, was a wheeler-dealer much like Lake himself. Under the terms of their agreement, Lake would hand over to the railroad magnate four hundred acres he had recently acquired (not surprisingly, the land was located adjacent to his bridge). In return, all Crocker had to do was agree to locate his depot on the property. The deal brought the railroad to Myron Lake, and the railroad, in turn, was blessed with a ready-made town site at its railhead. Promptly, Crocker divided Lake's acreage into four hundred choice lots (he immediately turned one hundred and twenty-seven of them back over to Lake); an auction was held; and, without hesitation, a city was laid out.

With the coming of the railroad, it was time for a change—particularly a name change. It was reasoned that the name "Lake's Crossing" was too long to be used on railroad timetables and too difficult for conductors to shout over the clatter of the wheels on steel. They had named a small community some eight miles to the west after Giuseppe Verdi, the famous opera composer (locals immediately decided that Ver-dye sounded better). Many thought that perhaps the town should be named Lincoln, after the martyred president.

Though many possible names were suggested, Crocker, a devout Union supporter, hit upon the name of an obscure Union general, Jesse L. Reno, who had been killed from ambush after a battle at South Mountain, Maryland, a few years before. Lake's Crossing overnight became Reno. The year was 1868. Wrote the *Carson City Appeal*, "Reno has sprung up feathered and lively. (Carson) must not let the new city on the Truckee run away with the capitol one of these days."

Still, Charles Crocker was not a man to take chances. He was determined to make sure that his newly created railhead would also enjoy a steady rate of growth. He offered fifty acres of land nearby to the family of the first child born in Reno. The following article soon appeared in the *Virginia City Territorial Enterprise*: "First birth in Reno! Today is recorded the birth of a daughter. The happy father, J. A. Carnahan, formerly of Virginia City, concluded to change his residence and having established himself, set out to do what any good citizen would do toward the improvement and advancement of the town. His 9-pound daughter is the first child born in the place and takes the real estate." The paper alluded subtly to the fact that Carnahan had moved to Reno just shortly before the birth and that Reno itself would never amount to much without such growth incentives.

Regardless, at the time the prediction of the newspaper was not far from being wrong. The majority of people entering the Truckee Meadows were still just passing through. To make matters worse, by 1869, after the completion of the railroad over the Sierra, the region was inundated by the very people who had made it possible—the Chinese who had built it. In that year one out of every four people in the region was Chinese, a fact

THE CITY'S NAMESAKE. *This early photo of General Jesse L. Reno was taken shortly before his death from ambush after a Civil War battle near South Mountain, Maryland. Although Reno had never been west, his name was selected as the replacement for Lake's Crossing because it was shorter and easier to use on railroad timetables. Photo courtesy of the Nevada Historical Society*

that threw the fledgling city into an uproar.

Prejudice was rampant. Governor Bradley worried publicly that the Chinese would erode the bright future of what people were, for the first time, calling the Silver State. Said the governor, "When the children know that Chinese boys can be procured so cheaply—a dollar a week—it is with great reluctance that the white children of Nevada will assist in household labors. If the presence of this cheap Chinese labor continues in our midst, thereby encouraging idleness among the white population, all the resources of the state will not furnish reformatory schoolhouses enough to hold, feed and clothe our hoodlum population." His concerns, of course, were unfounded. The frugal, hard-working Chinese simply continued to work for a mere pittance, without complaint, and so with the railroad they moved on.

By this time the lucrative business established by Myron Lake was on the decline. On New Year's Day, 1870, he opened a two-story hotel (the first of its kind in the region), but within two years, his profitable charter with

THE WINE HOUSE. *The Wine House on Commercial Row (shown here in an 1870s photograph) was one of the city's longest operating businesses. This site was* originally occupied by the Bender Bank, Reno's first financial institution. Photo courtesy of the Nevada Historical Society

the county of Washoe expired. Lake's bridge and toll road became toll-free. Furious, Lake put a gate across the bridge and, for a time, defended his rights with a six-shooter, but eventually he was forced to concede. Lake, now a wealthy man, sold his bridge to S. W. Kimball, who then erected a foundry on the site.

Reno was rapidly becoming the hub for the curious mass of humanity that was headed for the diggings. There were about two hundred and fifty buildings in the town, and newly arrived bankers in severely tailored suits rubbed elbows with flashy confidence men and land speculators. Teamsters, miners, and gamblers crowded the city streets. All major businesses faced the railroad depot, and soon a five-block stretch known as Commercial Row (comprised mainly of saloons and small hotels) had sprung up.

One handbill graphically illustrated that the new township was ready for anything. It read: "The Battery. It makes old men feel young and young men feel strong. Only a quarter of a dollar pays the bill. Nothing can be applied that is equal to it; it's one of nature's own remedies. Have your nervous system electrified!" The strange-looking device utilized an ominous assortment of wires and delivered a mild shock.

But electricity was already in the air. Speculators converged on the rail city and many, without once having visited the mines themselves, lay in wait for the unwitting tenderfeet who were arriving daily on the Central Pacific.

The magnates of the Comstock, however, were too busy mining to become involved in reckless speculation of the market. John Mackay, who by now was building a home in Reno, was quoted as saying:

I am not into speculating in the stock market. My business is mining, legitimate mining. I see that my men do their work properly and all goes as it should in the mills. I make my money here out of the ore.

Naturally, had I the desire to do so, I could go down to San Francisco with 10,000 shares of

*"THE STREETS ARE PAVED WITH MUD!" This 1874 Commercial Row street scene belies the fact that Reno was fast becoming Nevada's hub of commerce. Photo courtesy of the Nevada Historical Society*

stock in my pocket and by throwing it on the market at a critical moment, I could bring about a panic. But suppose I did that and made half a million by the job—what is that to me? By attending to my legitimate business here in Nevada, I can take that much out within a week.

Apparently the prudent Mackay practiced what he preached. When asked by a young businessman for investment advice, he replied, "What stocks should you buy? Buy nothing. Go and put your money in a savings bank instead!"

By 1871 politicians of the growing metropolis moved to wrest the county seat from Washoe City (at the time Nevada's second largest city). With the completion of a railroad spur—the Virginia and Truckee, which connected the Central Pacific with Carson City and the mines of the Comstock—the die was cast. On April 3, 1871, Reno became the county seat.

A place for a much-needed courthouse was donated by Myron Lake. Although the proposed location (still the site of the present courthouse) was bitterly contested as being too far south of the main part of town, Lake greased the wheels of government with $1500 as well as the land; the commissioners accepted.

Like most burgeoning towns of the West, the youthful Reno, Nevada, had its share of excitement, but the one ingredient sadly lacking was a female population. A brisk business in brides by mail sprang up, as evidenced by a letter to the venerable Alf Doten of Virginia City, who by now was spending more of his time in Reno. Wrote Madame E. F. Thornton of Hudson, New York, "The name of your future wife is Pauline Wegan and she is a merchant's daughter from Old Berlin, Illinois. She has a fine appearance, a kind disposition, an ardent temperament and is fond of home life." She enclosed a photograph

*THE HOTEL RENO. Patrons and staff of the Hotel Reno pose on the steps and balcony in 1901. After the decline of Virginia City's mines, many wondered if the dependent city could survive in the twentieth century. Photographer unknown*

*COMMERCIAL ROW IN THE 1870s.
As if to indicate the tremendous
importance of the railroad to the still-
growing community, all buildings faced the
tracks. Photo courtesy of Reno Orthopedic
Clinic*

of the woman as added proof of her claims. Doten, however, did not succumb to the temptation.

Not all of the women needed to be imported. Although history does not record most of their contributions in the early days of the city, Hannah Clapp was a difficult person to overlook. She arrived in 1859 when the area was still a part of the Utah Territory and for more than forty years she would champion two causes loudly and efficiently—women's rights and education. To Clapp, there was little that was beyond the realm of reform, from polygamy (which she scorned) to religion (which she seemed only to tolerate). At one point, determined that she was capable of doing any job as well as, if not better than, a man, she bid on and received the contract to construct an iron fence around the grounds of the State Capitol Building (that fence remains to this day). She was responsible for founding the Sierra Seminary and would later become one of the first faculty members in the city's new university.

Meanwhile, Reno was on the move. On November 23, 1870, the city's first true newspaper, the weekly *Nevada State Journal*, hit the streets. Its masthead included Lincoln's famous phrase: "With malice toward none, with

charity to all, and with firmness in the right." Far from heralding its own birth, the paper was content to feature such items as Bits of Fun ("The war is over in Europe—if not, where is it?"), Personal Items ("Julia Ward Howe has gone out of the Battle Hymn business, and wants peace"), and something called A String of Pearls ("Worldly pleasures are no more able to satisfy the soul than the light of a candle to give day to the world."). There was also a story on the dangers of New York City at night.

By the mid-1870s, freight cars had replaced the vast wagon trains and mule teams, and Reno had truly become the commercial hub of the region. But there were storm clouds on the horizon. Rumors were circulating that the wealth of the fabulous Comstock, on which Reno desperately depended, was fading.

ON C STREET,
VIRGINIA CITY, NEV.

E.F. SHAW.

*POST CARD STATUS. When this picture
was taken of Virginia City after the turn of
the century, the boom was over. Although
the city still maintained a gallant profile, it
was merely a shadow of its former self,
having lost more than two-thirds of its population. Photo courtesy of Bennett Photos*

# A Shifting Of Power:
# The Rush Toward The Twentieth Century

In the final quarter of the nineteenth century, Reno, Nevada, had but one real goal: to survive during the impending decline of the Comstock. For a region dependent primarily on mineral wealth, it would be a difficult period at best, but the realization was slow in coming.

While Virginia City was still a household word in much of the nation, Reno remained little more than a wide spot in the road. In 1877, luxury-loving magazine owner Frank Leslie hired a private train for what his popular tabloid referred to as an "Excursion to the Pacific." For five months the editor moved across the country—from Chicago to Cheyenne, from Denver to Salt Lake, and on into San Francisco—treating his readers to colorful copy and detailed illustrations. Though he gave considerable space to both Virginia City and the state capital at Carson, Reno itself merited but a few lines. It was merely the place where he changed trains.

Nonetheless, private business thrived during the 1870s. Small shops and stores sprung up offering "the finest accoutrements to be found east of San Francisco!" The three-story, two-block long Depot Hotel was the city's finest hostelry and showplace—greeting arrivals with treatment that glistened with an image of wealth and accomplishment. The moment a newcomer stepped from the train there was little doubt that this was a city to be reckoned with.

A Reno tailor, Jacob W. Davis, would become wealthy, although few would realize his accomplishments at the time. The ingenious Davis had fashioned a pair of pants for a burly woodcutter. Made from rugged tent canvas and reinforced with copper rivets, the kind commonly used in making horse blankets, the pants soon proved to be popular, especially among the men in the mines. Soon Davis's business was booming. The sudden influx of orders attracted the attention of his supplier, Levi Strauss

of San Francisco. A meeting followed, and a patent was issued jointly in their names. The blue jean dynasty was born.

Lawlessness was rampant during the early years. When justice faltered, the earliest citizenry relied on the mysterious members of the "601," or Committee of Vigilance, which had banded together to help the city rid itself of the seedy assortment of thieves, vagrants, and other low-lifes. At first, they simply "invited" suspected wrongdoers to leave town. If that didn't work, more forceful methods were employed, such as the popular use of tar and feathers.

The "601" was active for almost thirty years, but its most notorious contribution to law and order came in 1891, when a would-be tough named Luis Ortiz became the guest of honor at a "601" necktie party. Ortiz had been arrested after a shooting spree that had left several people seriously wounded. Deciding to save the county of Washoe the time and expense of a trial, members of the committee assembled at the courthouse. Under cover of darkness they hustled the trembling Ortiz from his cell and dragged him to the nearby Virginia Street Bridge. It was there that the grisly corpse was discovered the following morning, dangling eerily inches above the Truckee River. It was a grim public reminder to others who dared to defy law and order. But still many did.

At well past midnight on a blustery November night in 1870, Central Pacific engine No. 1 had begun the last leg of its long journey from Oakland, California, to Reno. Though two hours behind schedule, the crew could finally relax. Just ahead was the town of Verdi, and the worst of the haul was over.

Suddenly, from out of the darkness appeared six masked and armed men. Leaping aboard the slowly moving train, they ordered the engine to a stop. After uncoupling the passenger coaches from the express car,

THE "HANGING" BRIDGE. Under the cover of darkness and without the benefit of a trial, ruffian Luis Ortiz was taken from his jail cell by members of the "601," a vigilante group that was prominent in the West. When Reno citizens awoke, they found his body dangling eerily above the Truckee River. Drawing courtesy of the Nevada Historical Society

FRONTIER JUSTICE. The body of William "Red" Wood hangs from a telegraph pole, the only convenient structure in the vast open space surrounding the tiny community of Hazen in 1905. Photo courtesy of the Nevada Historical Society

they pulled away, only to halt once more a few miles down the line at a deserted quarry near Lawton Hot Springs. Disarming the express messenger and locking up the crew, they hacked open the express box and found a small fortune—a payroll shipment of forty-one thousand dollars in gold coins destined for the mines of Virginia City. Stuffing the money into some old boots lashed to their saddles, they mounted their horses and galloped off into the night. They had pulled off the first train robbery in the West.

The robbers did not have long to enjoy their success. The following morning, at daybreak, Undersheriff Jim Kinkead organized a posse. Within two days, the men had two of the robbers in custody. Learning that another was hiding at a farm near Sierraville, Kinkead, now alone, rode on through the night. The following morning he returned with the man in custody.

In the meantime, county authorities had learned the identities of the remainder of the gang. By the close of the week, all of the robbers were in jail and all but three thousand dollars of the money was recovered.

As a rail city, Reno had long before tied its future, not to gold or silver, but to commerce, and there were many who concluded that the decision was foolhardy. The town was at the mercy, quite literally, of its own mentor, the Central Pacific Railroad.

It was expensive to ship goods to the fledgling city. For example, if a would-be supplier wanted to move freight from New York to San Francisco, the price was about six hundred dollars a carload. To ship those same goods to Reno, however, the price rose by 33 percent, to eight hundred dollars, even though Reno was actually en route and the distance was considerably shorter.

This practice was common throughout the West during the 1870s and 1880s. Called "back hauling," the procedure brought angry headlines and an outcry from public officials. Said Nevada's lone congressman, "Nevada is an orange which these railroad vampires have been sucking in silence. Their object is to crush, not to develop the industries of Nevada."

The Central Pacific was notoriously late in paying its taxes as well. Aware that Reno needed the railroad more than the railroad needed the city, officials deliberately delayed in the payment of land-use taxes to Washoe County. But a young deputy sheriff (the same Jim Kinkead who had orchestrated the capture of the area's first train robbers), who would go on to become one of the state's most famous lawmen, had a solution. He simply waited until the next locomotive steamed into the depot. Once the engine had been pulled to a siding, he moved in with a length of logging chain and secured it to the tracks. Within a week, Kinkead had not one, but three engines immobilized in Reno, and soon the Central Pacific got the message. They wired their bank to pay the back taxes and interest without further delay.

The railroad was indelibly linked to Reno's future. On the evening of June 3, 1876, the entire town turned out to witness the arrival of the Jarrett and Palmer Lightning Train. It was a centennial year for America, and what had begun as a coast-to-coast publicity stunt soon became an all-out race to break the speed record for the run between New York and San Francisco. When the train pulled into the Reno stop, it was greeted by brass bands and considerable flag waving. "Day by day the annihilation of time and space is becoming perfected," predicted a reporter. "The American Continent can now be safely crossed at the incredible speed of 45 miles an hour!" he crowed.

Another newspaper began publication in 1876. The competitor, the *Reno Evening Gazette*, took advantage of the growing population and offered a daily, which could be ordered at the annual subscription rate of $10. The following year, in an attempt to go head-on-head with the weekly *Journal*, the *Gazette* offered a weekly of its own, which appeared on Saturdays.

It was during this time that a strapping two-hundred-and-thirty-pound Reno blacksmith began to make a name for himself. Born on the rocky Cornish coast, Richard Jose was the eldest of five children. Upon the death of his father, he was sent to live with an uncle in Virginia City. The youngster, blessed with an exceptionally pleasing voice, took to entertaining in the saloons along the burgeoning C Street until Temperance League members complained. The lad was quickly sent off to a boarding school in Reno where he soon found employment as a blacksmith's apprentice.

Though he grew to be a giant in stature, his voice, as he matured, retained its pure tenor quality and Jose was offered a job with a traveling minstrel show. His popularity continued, blossoming into a national tour which culminated with a New York concert at the world-famous Carnegie Hall. He toured as "Reno's Blacksmith Balladeer" and after the turn of the century he joined Enrico Caruso as one of the featured artists for the new Victor Talking Machine. He would go on to win national fame for his adopted city, making such songs as "Silver Threads Among the Gold" popular classics.

While the future was looking bright for Reno, on the Comstock the doomsayers were predicting the depletion of the mines with increasing regularity. In 1880, in a particularly lackadaisical whistlestop speech, President Rutherford B. Hayes sagely urged residents to "protect themselves from raucous living for Good Health is a treasure beyond all price."

Hayes's words went unheeded. Reno still felt it was on a roll, and progress, thought many, had come to the Truckee Meadows to stay.

City living, however, still left a lot to be desired. Virginia Street, the main thoroughfare leading south from the railroad depot, was little more than a crudely graded quagmire. So treacherous was the bustling street that in 1871 local merchants hired a work crew to remove the rocks over which people were constantly stumbling. Spools of barbed wire, placed in front of many business establishments to keep horses and other stray animals from entering, were commonplace. Adding to the morass was the smell of the slaughterhouses and stockyards located nearby. As the Washoe zephyrs combed the Meadows in late afternoon, a horrendous odor permeated the business district. Despite the air of optimism that clung tenaciously to the mining industry, by 1876 most of Reno's seventeen hundred people were still living in rustic squalor.

*BIGGER THAN THE COMSTOCK!*
*Although it was not to be, Nevada's mining*
*industry in 1898 still hoped that more*
*remained of the fabulous Comstock Lode.*
*Note the Chinese workman at top row*

*center. The Chinese were not allowed to*
*work the mines during Virginia City's*
*heyday. Photo courtesy of the Nevada*
*Historical Society*

Still a sense of identity had begun to emerge. Author William Rowley in his book *Reno: the Hub of Washoe County* recalled:

Reno's first baseball club, the Reno Stars, was organized in June 1871; the Reno Glee Club followed in September. In 1875 on the south side of the river and one mile east of Reno, 40 acres of land was designated as the County Poor Farm. A year later a contract was drawn up for the construction of a county hospital on the property. A building for performances appeared when L. H. Dyer opened the first theater in 1871 to attract some of the larger acting companies heading for the Comstock.

Fire, the scourge of every new town, broke out with frightening regularity. On October 29, 1873, flames engulfed the Western Hotel, located on Commercial Row between Virginia and Sierra streets. Soon the entire block was burning, and within minutes the city's business

district was a raging inferno in which more than one hundred buildings would be destroyed.

The next day in a special edition, the *Journal* reported: "The citizens turned out en masse and battled with the fiery element as only men will battle when they see their all going to destruction. Wet blankets were brought out and laid on the roofs of adjoining houses, but to no purpose." A history of Reno's fire department written in 1908 recalled that fire units from the Central Pacific railroad yards in Truckee and Wadsworth were on the scene, as well as engines from Carson City. They were painfully helpless.

The next day the *Journal* soberly concluded, "In the excitement and confusion now prevailing, it is utterly impossible to form a correct estimate of the value of property lost." But it added optimistically, "We desire to state that Reno will rise Phoenix-like and be better and brighter than ever before. The businessmen of Reno are true, good men. They are men of energy and ability, and though they may not all be men of capital, they have that which will make capital—hard muscles and a spirit which knows no such word as fail."

But history would soon repeat itself. Early on Sunday morning, March 2, 1879, sparks from a nearby chimney landed on the roof of the Hagerman and Schooling Store on Sierra Street. Reported members of the fire brigade:

Four hours the fire raged, carrying everything before it, only stopping when there was nothing left in its tracks to consume. The greater portion of 10 blocks were destroyed.

When the fire had burned itself out a barren waste was all that was left to mark the spot where a few hours before a beautiful, thriving town had its existence.

So disastrous was the blaze that the state legislature immediately appropriated one thousand dollars in relief funds for the stricken city, and surrounding towns rushed to assist. The *Nevada State Journal* stated: "Virginia and Carson volunteered aid and on Sunday night sent carloads of food and bedding and thousands of dollars in money. Kind offers of aid came from Sacramento, San Francisco and other cities thick and fast."

Grieved the *Journal*, "The mournful fact is patent that it will be a long time before Reno will again be the fair city she was less than a week ago. She will recover in time but will be retarded in the race for many a year." Nonetheless, within a week the city was rebuilding, with lots in the decimated business district bringing one hundred dollars per front foot.

It took but a few years before the devastating effects of the conflagration were forgotten and the city had risen again from the ashes. Two ads appearing in the *Daily Journal*, dated August 10, 1884, indicated that the town was ripe for anything. "Dr. Minte, Specialist and Graduate," blared one, "treats all chronic, special and private diseases with wonderful success. The great English remedy is a certain cure for Lost Manhood and all of the evil effects of youthful follies and excess!"

Another ad, perhaps a forerunner of the modern cereal-box giveaways, boasted: "$11,950 in Cash Given Away!" All the winners had to do was collect the most number of premiums from Blackwell's Genuine Bull Durham Smoking Tobacco.

Gambling was prevalent in Reno during the period, as it was in most mining towns across the frontier. The back rooms and alleyways along Commercial Row were dotted with assorted faro tables, as those waiting for trains to Virginia City and Carson whiled away the hours.

But the serious gamblers spent most of their time at the town's racetrack. So popular was the sport that both of the city's papers ran daily results in prominent locations. The track, located near the site of today's Livestock Equestrian Center, brought in such added attractions as Professor Price's Balloon Ascension, an event that brought crowds from miles around. Other forms of gambling

THE CITY BOASTS PUBLIC TRANSPORTATION. A new trolley car passes in front of Republican headquarters on Second Street. Although some horse-drawn vehicles can still be seen in this 1907 photograph, the horseless carriage was fast becoming a regular sight on the city's streets. Photo courtesy of Jean C. Hubbard

*READIN', WRITIN', 'RITHMETIC.*
*This photograph taken in the late 1800s*
*shows the Anderson School, the city's*
*oldest. Photo courtesy of the Kleppe family*

hardly made a ripple in the papers. The big news was the University of Nevada in Reno. With considerable pride, the city fathers pointed to the fact that the original university, which had been organized in far-off Elko in 1874, had been moved to the rail city the very next year. The undertaking was particularly notable due to the fact that many of the actual buildings had been moved as well—a tremendous accomplishment for the time. By 1887, the University of Nevada, now in Reno, was well established.

In the *Evening Gazette* on September 28, banner headlines heralded the accomplishments of the fledgling school and featured a biography of the new president, Leroy Brown. While it failed to mention that the military-trained Brown was a strict disciplinarian who was generally disliked by the students, it did publish the names of those who had enrolled—all forty-five of them. The article went on to state proudly that three departments would be offered: "Business"—including spelling, reading, writing, and arithmetic, history, bookkeeping and the use

of the typewriter, "Normal"—a course for aspiring teachers which featured such subjects as the history of education and the school laws of Nevada, and "Academic"—which offered, primarily, training in those careers directly related to the mining industry—chemistry, geology, and mineralogy.

It was a period of growth and prosperity. By 1890 Reno was calling itself the "Healthiest Town in Nevada!" and for good reason. Electric lighting had been in place for more than three years. The city even boasted of having a streetcar line that linked the business and residential districts.

Regardless of the fact that civilization had finally arrived, residents were still at the mercy of the elements and the winter of 1889-1890 would prove disastrous.

It had begun innocently enough. First the weather turned cold and the winds angry. There were skating parties, bonfires, and sledding down the hill from the new university. Old-timers chuckled as the children gleefully romped and played. As the year came to a close, few were laughing any longer.

"Cuss words are the order of the day," the newspaper said. But to many even cussing didn't help. A lot of people in the Truckee Meadows were freezing, and some of them to death. The city fathers ordered the water pipes to be wrapped in woolen blankets to keep them from bursting in the sub-zero temperatures, which sometimes dipped to thirty degrees below.

Not even the railroad could get through. By mid-January, more than six hundred westbound passengers on the Central Pacific had been stranded in Reno. With lodging at a premium, Pullman cars were converted into sleeping rooms. Coal from the tenders was stolen by ingenious children sent out to fill their pockets with the precious fuel.

Yet there was humor, too, among the stricken. An East Coast newspaper editor, George McCully, printed a small pamphlet called "Snowbound: A Souvenir of the Sierra Nevada Blockade" and sales were brisk. Railroad Vice President J. C. Stubbs, embarrassed by the inability of his line to make it over the mountains, trudged nightly through the whiteness to lecture on "The Cussedness of the Elements."

Things were far worse on the open range. Cattle by the thousands perished, their carcasses frozen upright and crusted with eerie, glistening crystal. As their livelihood agonizingly ebbed away before their eyes, ranchers could do little but stand helplessly by and wait.

By January 30, 1890, the storm finally subsided and Reno was once again linked with the rest of the world. Only then was the true magnitude of the storm realized. Northwest of the city, the Sparks-Tinnan Ranch, which had branded more than forty-two thousand calves the year before, branded less than fifty that spring.

Reporter Alf Doten tried valiantly to make light of the situation. Wrote Doten, "20 years hence liars will undoubtedly glory in tales of 50-foot snow drifts and how everyone traveled over the tops of houses on snowshoes. Old timers always exaggerate." But about the deadly winter of 1889-1890, Doten was wrong. It would be the worst winter in the city's history.

Still, the town was slowly becoming established. In a poorly spelled advertisement dated March 24, 1896, lots along the Truckee River were being offered for what many considered exorbitant prices. "RENO REAL ESTATE BRGAINS!" roared the headline. "Choicest and Cheapest Lots for Cash or on the Installment Plan." For six hundred to one thousand dollars, readers could take advantage of "The South Side of the Truckee River!" which had "always been the favorite site for homes and many of the best residences of Reno have been constructed there." The ad went on to explain that "the Riverside Hotel Lots, facing the river, are now on the market and as they are only a few, first come will be first served." The paper hastily added, "It is worthy of the thought that this valuable tract should have been kept intact for 25 years." Myron Lake, the region's first real estate investor, was probably smiling.

Not everyone felt that Reno real estate was overpriced.

*NO DROUGHT HERE. The Truckee River rages past this row of fine homes just after the turn of the century. Photo courtesy of Ethel Warren*

Millionaire Francis G. Newlands, who had made his fortune through his association with Comstock magnate William Sharon and whose daughter he had married, moved to Reno in 1871 and built a fine home surrounded by orchards on land overlooking the river. The fact that such a prominent and wealthy man had chosen to move to Reno raised the spirits of local businessmen considerably.

It was Newlands who first suggested that Reno should take great pains to conserve its water. When local officials failed to heed his suggestions for the building of reservoirs upstream, Newlands himself procured the site, including Donner Lake. Though the city concluded that its priorities were elsewhere, Newlands himself was undaunted. Despite his failure to enlist support for the project, he went on to become a congressman in 1892 and was elevated to the Senate a decade later.

As the century neared its close, it was the mining industry that continued to dominate the news. A brief political movement advocated the unlimited production of silver coins in the hope that the concept would allow many of Nevada's mines to reopen. It was not to be. The platform went down in defeat with the presidential election of 1896. A feeling of gloom and uncertainty was blanketing the Truckee Meadows.

By the late 1880s most of the fabulous wealth of the Comstock had disappeared. There were new strikes being reported almost daily in far-off, still unnamed parts of the state, but the city that had been priding itself for being the "center of the universe" was sadly in decline.

Wrote editor Wells Drury:

Virginia City now lies stricken and old. The mountainside which shook and echoed with the stamps of a score of mills is silent. A few of the old timers linger on, a C Street sign seeks pathetically to keep up the show despite the grim staring ruins of the old Wells Fargo Building. The churches alone stand staunch and unshaken.

Above, on the slopes of Mount Davidson, are rows of ramshackled wooden buildings, some of them 4 stories high, leaning against each other in desolate insecurity. A Washoe zephyr might huff and puff and blow them down like a house of cards. Most of the houses which clung to the slopes in this fair city were torn down long ago, often board by board and used for firewood. Tis sad indeed. So passes the glory of the Comstock.

Reno was suffering from the effect. Although figures vary, during the heyday of the Comstock, it was estimated that more than sixty thousand people were living in the shadow of Davidson. By 1880, more than twenty thousand had left in search of greener pastures. A census taken during that same year indicated that there were only sixty-two thousand residents in the entire state of Nevada and fully one-quarter of that number were still living in the area of Virginia City, Gold Hill, and Silver City. Adding to the sense of gloom was news of an even more fabulous strike in Juneau, Alaska.

By the end of the century, while the rest of the West was building, Nevada seemed to be shrinking. As the year 1900 approached, the state's population dropped even further—to 42,300.

Still, there were those who contended that the future would be bright. In 1898 the Reno Improvement Society (forerunner of the Greater-Reno Sparks Chamber of Commerce) was formed.

But to many, it seemed like the rush to riches and a bright future was over. It was grimly noted that Reno had not yet bothered to incorporate as a city.

*THE GRANDEUR OF CASAZZA DRIVE. This picture of a three-story residence was taken by an unknown photographer in the early 1900s. The home occupied the present location of Shopper's Square.*

*A FAMILY PORTRAIT. Members of the pioneering Kleppe family pose for the photographer. Note the fashionable identical hairstyles on the women. Photo courtesy of the Kleppe family*

*SHARING THE LOAD—TAMING THE LAND. Spring planting on the Kleppe Ranch in 1915. Both men and women worked side by side in the fields to till the harsh Nevada Land. Photo courtesy of the Kleppe family*

*CENTER OF COMMERCE. This scene of Commercial Row, just after the turn of the century, shows the tremendous growth that had taken place. A sign in the foreground, placed strategically for the benefit of speculators arriving by rail, trumpets Reno's new Educational Center. Photo courtesy of the Reno Orthopedic clinic*

# The Turn Of The Century: A Coming Of Age

*Reno is dull because its roots—socially, humanly speaking—are fastened in decay. If you like to put it that way, Reno is sinister. This little town with its girdle of enchanting mountains, its wide well-kept streets, its delightful park where the Truckee River flows—irrigation creating for it a dense greenness in the midst of the hopeless desert— has a fairly equivocal future. Its past is the past of the great mining camps. It was bred in their tradition.*

*The Reno magnates are men who knew and took their part in the earlier hectic days—sinking into old age and death now, squandering or saving their "piles," but without any prospect of more "piles" to be made. The gold and silver, you see, have gone. Even the Comstock Lode petered out.*

*It must never be forgotten that the human habit of Reno are the tradition, the point of view, the human habit of a mining camp. A mining camp after the gold is gone is not a cheerful or an exciting place. The big men, the great adventurers go and only the little men and the habit of gambling for lessening stakes are left . . .*

So wrote roving author Katherine Geroald back in 1925. In 1900 many residents were already murmuring many of the same thoughts.

As the new century dawned, many Renoites felt stranded, almost isolated; while all around them, envied new bonanzas were springing up. Indeed, the big news as 1900 rolled around was the discovery of an incredible new strike in Tonopah far to the southeast. As if to add insult to injury, just two years later the cry of riches came again, this time from a place called Goldfield.

Automobiles had by now replaced pack animals on the trek across the desert, but the strike at Goldfield seemed destined to dwarf even the fabulous Comstock. Colorful characters like Tex Rickard, who had made a fortune in the gold fields of the Klondike and then promptly lost it again, had opened the Northern Saloon which was being touted as "the grand-daddy" of them all. As if to defy the imagination, the establishment boasted a fifty-foot bar ("The longest in the west!") and it was worked feverishly by two dozen bartenders each shift. The elegant Palace Shaving Parlour, operated by J. J. Noone, featured fourteen chairs and was heralded as the finest "west of the

Mississippi and east of San Francisco!" Even the legendary Wyatt Earp called Goldfield home. It seemed that Nevada's growth had passed Reno by for a second time.

In truth, however, the city was making progress in other ways. During the first decade of the twentieth century, the population of Reno had more than doubled, to more than ten thousand by 1910. Congressman Newlands had succeeded nationally in what he had merely attempted to accomplish in his hometown: to bring water to the desert. The National Reclamation Act passed in 1902 and the following year an ambitious federal project was initiated in nearby Fallon.

The tiny burst of optimism was further fanned when, in 1903, after considerable lobbying by local businessmen, Reno was awarded city status by the state legislature. Prior to this time, all major governing decisions had been made by county commissioners who had the power to levy taxes, pass ordinances, and even regulate the city's police and fire departments. Corruption was rampant.

Reno, with typical frontier reluctance in adapting to change, opted for the traditional mayoral type of government and elected D. W. O'Conner as the city's first

*DOWN RIVER. This view of the Truckee River looks east around 1907. Note the trolley on the Virginia Street Bridge. Photo courtesy of Jean C. Hubbard*

*RENO HIGH CHAMPS. Football was as popular in early area schools as it was on the university campus. Here members of the Reno High School football team pose for a photograph in 1900. Photo courtesy of Ethel Warren*

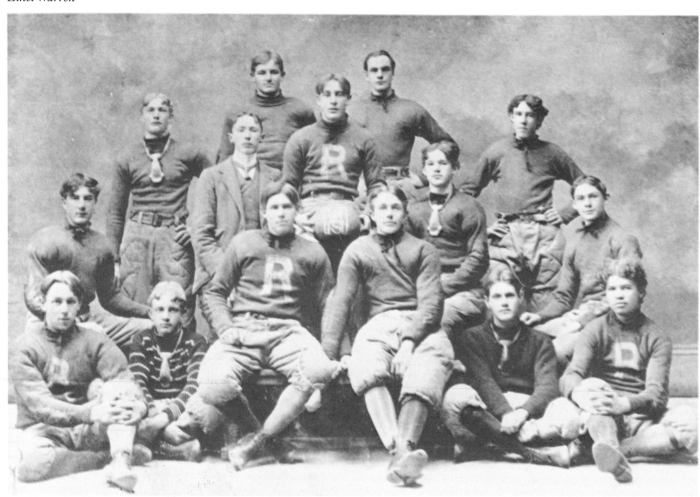

*NCORY. The Nevada-California-Oregon Railway building on Fourth Street (circa 1910). Photo courtesy of Jean C. Hubbard*

mayor. The town was divided into major geographical areas, and representatives were chosen to form the first city council.

As the new era dawned, it looked for a time like the city was destined to become a major manufacturing center. Electric companies had invested heavily in miles of wooden aqueducts, much of which can still be seen today. Diverting the raging waters of the Truckee precariously along the canyon walls to power stations at Farad and Verdi, it seemed at first that inexpensive power would soon set a new direction for the region. Bolstered by high hopes, the Reno Milling and Flour Company and the Riverside Mill sprang up.

But raw materials were still scarce, labor was expensive, and to a great degree (due primarily to word of the almost-daily new mineral discoveries filtering in from the desert) in short supply. Adding to the lack of direction was the railroad, which still held the city in its grasp.

In 1904 the following advertisement appeared in *Sunset Magazine*: "There are plenty of opportunities for the homeowner, the manufacturer and the investor. Don't miss it!" The ad was promoting the virtues, not of Reno,

but of the new town of Harriman located just a stone's throw to the east (for years the main headquarters for the Southern Pacific and the Central Pacific before it had been located in the town of Wadsworth). The announcement came as a surprise to many, for the town had not even existed before the ad appeared.

In a cost-cutting measure, officials decided to straighten out the rails a bit, bypass the town of Wadsworth entirely, and then build a new railhead a little closer to creature comforts. They proposed to literally uproot the entire town of Wadsworth and move it—lock, stock, and barrel.

The citizens of Wadsworth were incensed. For years, the city had thrived along with the railroad. Pick up the town and move it? The idea, to most, was heresy. But officials of the Southern Pacific were determined.

They did, however, make the residents of Wadsworth an offer. They agreed to give each person willing to relocate a choice 50 by 140 foot lot right next to the new roundhouse with the provision that a home be built within a year. The idea caught on. Handbills and newspaper ads appeared with offers of "Free Homesites!" and soon workers were

49

*THE RAIL CITY. The endless Nevada desert stretches beyond the east end of Commercial Row just after 1900. Soon the city of Sparks would spring up, becoming a rail center for the powerful Central Pacific. Photo courtesy of the Reno Orthopedic Clinic*

*ALL ABOARD! Passengers scurry aboard as the Overland Limited leaves Reno from the Southern Pacific depot around 1910. Photo courtesy of Jean C. Hubbard*

*THEY NAMED A CITY AFTER HIM.*
*Governor John Sparks, after whom the city*
*of Sparks was named, sits astride his*
*favorite horse. An avid rancher and*
*sportsman, Sparks would entertain*
*reporters and public officials on his lavish*
*spread northeast of Reno. Photo courtesy of*
*the Nevada Historical Society*

joined by land speculators, bunko artists, and investors who lined up for free land in "an infant city of untold wealth!"

A drawing was conducted; names of prospective property owners in one hat, lot numbers in another. Before long more than sixty lots had been awarded.

In Wadsworth, buildings, homes, and even trees were uprooted and placed on flatcars for transport to the new site. The Southern Pacific had done it. They succeeded in creating a thriving railhead right where they wanted it. It had happened almost overnight.

Investors, however, wanted a name change. They wanted something that extolled the unlimited virtues of the new city, a name that bespoke wealth and opportunity, something like "Golden," "Silverton," or "Heavenly."

Church groups, on the other hand, wanted something more reserved. Still others suggested the name East Reno. Reno's *Daily Journal* ran a contest to choose the new moniker and even offered a whopping ten dollar first prize. Among the finalists: Essau, Carsage, and again, East Reno.

In the end, it was decided to name the fledgling city after Nevada's popular governor, John Sparks, who regularly (and lavishly!) entertained on his ranch and hunting preserve a few miles to the north. Sparks pooh-poohed the suggestion, saying in a letter to the selection committee that he did not feel the idea was "appropriate." Just the same, Harriman was renamed the city of Sparks.

The newspaper wrote in glowing terms, "Naturally like all new towns, Sparks possesses its due portion of saloons. There is no more room for more places of that kind

*WINGFIELD ON THE RUN. In the aftermath of the disastrous San Francisco earthquake, Reno entrepreneur George Wingfield was satirized in print. Caught unaware in the debacle, the banker was forced to run from his hotel room clad only in his undershorts. Wingfield was unharmed and hardly destitute. Somehow he had managed to escape with more than forty thousand dollars sewn into the lining of his underwear. Courtesy of the Nevada Historical Society*

*THE PRIDE OF THE CITY. The Reno Wheelmen, shown here in a 1901 program, was a popular bicycle relay team. Wherever they appeared, huge crowds lined the streets to cheer them on. Courtesy of the Nevada Historical Society*

here. It may be said however that the saloons of Sparks are better conducted and kept in a more orderly manner than those of almost any town in the west. The absense of crime here in Sparks is truly remarkable." Even though few realized it at the time, the struggling city of Reno now had competition right next door.

In 1906 disaster struck. The great San Francisco earthquake occurred hundreds of miles away, yet it sent shockwaves through the entire state of Nevada—causing panic in the mining industry which, even at the best of times, was precarious.

George Wingfield, one of the state's leading financiers, was staying at the Palace Hotel when the first tremor came. Although he was forced from the hostelry without his pants and had to wrap himself in a woman's skirt, he managed to escape the holocaust with more than forty thousand dollars wisely sewn into his undershorts. He quickly headed back to Tonopah in a desperate attempt to quell the impending panic.

In Tonopah and Goldfield, the brokerage houses immediately shut down, and meetings were held to organize relief efforts which brought three thousand dollars from Manhattan and five thousand dollars from both Rhyolite and Tonopah. Contingents from the latter personally set up shelters for the homeless in the ruins of San Francisco.

Nevada's mining industry was also violently shaken by the ferocity of the quake. In an attempt to calm the fears of Eastern financial interests, investor Charles Schwab stepped forward in a generous offer to personally guarantee the trembling stocks in Tonopah. His efforts brought only temporary relief. Months after the quake, many brokerage houses remained closed and some banks were operating only on a limited basis. Mining in Nevada would never fully recover.

Souvenir Program
GARDEN . CITY
vs
RENO . WHEELMEN
Sunday, July 17, 1904          Reno, Nevada

WILLIAM H. HART

Cigars                    Stationery

The...Model...
H. DAVIS

Quinn.....

Commercial Row          Virginia Street          Dentist

*THE EPITOME OF MASCULINITY.*
*The city's popular cycling team, the*
*Wheelmen, pose in their competition*
*finery. Courtesy of the Nevada Historical*
*Society*

In Reno, however, the city was basking in a new feeling of identity, much of it centering on sports. In 1900 Reno's prominent bicycle club, the Wheelmen, had succeeded in winning the prestigious Pacific Coast Championship racing meet. When the group returned to Reno in triumph, a crowd of more than three thousand turned out in jubilant celebration.

The city was about to enter the air age as well. Initially cut off from air travel by the towering Sierra, the problem was solved by bringing a "daring flying machine" to Reno crated in a box. Pilot Ivy Baldwin had managed to get one rickety craft off the ground in Carson City in 1910, but it would be two years before Reno could boast "Nevada's Biggest Flying Meet!"

Frank Bryant and Roy Francis, two California aces who had raced bicycles and automobiles on the carnival circuit before switching to aircraft, had brought two small planes to Reno by rail. On June 17, mechanics began to assemble the biplanes at Moana Springs at the southern edge of town.

Bryant, concerned that his tiny engine would be unable to generate sufficient thrust in Reno's rarefied atmosphere, decided to conduct a test. He borrowed a hanging-weight scale from a local meat packer, staked it down in the middle of a field and connected it by cable to his airplane. His worst fears were confirmed. His engine was underpowered. He wired to San Francisco and within hours ten gallons of a new experimental high-test fuel were placed aboard the Southern Pacific.

Filling his tank with the prototype mixture, Bryant's plane roared off down the dusty road and miraculously began to rise. But the experiment was short-lived. The aircraft climbed to a mere two hundred feet before dropping again into a wheat field owned by Dan Wheeler. A broken spark plug was the culprit.

On June 21, Bryant tried again. After nearly missing a stand of trees, he headed north toward Reno where crowds poured into the streets and pointed skyward. He circled the city to a wildly cheering population before returning again to Moana Springs.

*THE INVENTION OF THE CENTURY ARRIVES! This biplane, piloted by Roy Francis, prepares for takeoff during the Moana Springs Aviation Meet in Reno (June 1912). Photo courtesy of Frank M. Steinheimer*

Two days later, the now-confident daredevils really put their biplanes through their paces. An awestruck throng watched as the men rose to the incredible height of one thousand feet, then twenty-five hundred. As they crossed back and forth above the clamoring mass of humanity, they dropped handbills to the cheering crowd and then sailed back through them as they fluttered to the ground. It was the first demonstration of flight in the Truckee Meadows.

But it would be prizefighting that would truly put Reno on the map. On the Fourth of July, 1910, more than thirty thousand people surged into the city to witness the contest between the heavyweight champion of the world, Jack Johnson, and a man many were calling the "great white hope," Jim Jeffries. As the fighters made their way into the ring, carpenters were still driving spikes into the twenty-thousand-seat stadium that had been constructed on Fourth Street specifically for the event. So new was the construction that ticket holders would later complain that they were forced to sit in still-oozing pine pitch.

The entire city was enthralled. Crowds lined the roads from Johnson's training camp at Rick's Resort near Verdi and Jeffries' at Moana Hot Springs. People jammed the new Majestic Theater on the off chance that they might catch a glimpse of themselves in something called "newsreels."

The contest itself was the brainchild of Tex Rickard, the same entrepreneur who had parlayed his Goldfield investments into riches. He knew the staggering potential of professional boxing, for he had seen the popularity of the fight between Bob Fitzsimmons and "Gentleman Jim" Corbett in Carson City in 1897. He decided to become the black champion's manager.

With a finesse that would make P. T. Barnum pale with envy, Rickard sent Mrs. Johnson (amazingly enough, a white woman in a time of incredible prejudice) a mink coat. Having thus piqued the champion's interest, he followed with a personal invitation for Johnson to join him in a night on the town. After the two had managed to drink their way through most of the evening, Rickard dropped an envelope in front of Johnson. It contained $2,500 in hundred-dollar bills. The champion signed immediately.

Location was still a problem. Originally the fight had been scheduled for San Francisco, but Johnson's interracial marriage and his penchant for carousing outraged many in the city. Bending to the overwhelming public pressure, San Francisco withdrew as a possible site. Suddenly other towns were bidding feverishly for a chance to host the action.

Once again, the wily Rickard had an ace up his sleeve, and he certainly knew how to get people's attention. In a meeting in Hoboken, New Jersey, while others vying for the fight came merely prepared to make a bid, Rickard appeared with a satchel. Magnanimously dumping its contents out on the table, he counted out $100,000 in cash. Tex Rickard would bring the fight to Reno.

BOXING'S GREATEST TRAIN IN
LUXURY. *The Moana Baths was a
favorite of locals, but the luxury
accommodations were also shared by
champion prizefighters. Jim Jeffries,
dubbed the "Great White Hope," trained
here in preparation for his bout with Jack
Johnson. He should have trained harder.
Postcard courtesy of Frances Brisbin*

THE FIGHT OF THE CENTURY.
*Bettors gather in front of the official
headquarters for the Johnson-Jeffries bout
on July 3, 1910. Jack Johnson would defeat
Jim Jeffries in Reno's first and largest title
fight. The event attracted a record crowd of
more than twenty thousand spectators,
making it Reno's first special event. Photo
courtesy of Edwin Bender*

*VOTE FOR WOMEN. Citizens for Women's Suffrage campaign in the summer of 1914. Photo courtesy of the Bancroft Library, University of California-Berkeley.*

The event focused nationwide attention on the city. The transcontinental telephone line was still four years in the future, so wire services were set up and carrier pigeons were brought in as a backup. Special railroad cars were commandeered and converted into hotel rooms. A bath, when it could be had at all (often in water three days old), brought three dollars.

The newspapers across the country had a field day. They called the bout, "The fight to end all fights!" and claimed it was "the focal point of all things terrestrial!" Reno itself was referred to as the "precise magnetic center of the civilized world!"

The betting was heavy. One San Francisco man would wager $30,000 on the aging Jeffries, and a Los Angeles syndicate bet $50,000 on Johnson. The gate topped a quarter of a million dollars, more than twice the money brought in by the entire five-day World Series of that year. Promoter Rickard pocketed $135,000, enabling him to go on to handle such illustrious fighters as Jack Dempsey, whom he had met in the mining camps and who would eventually become the "Toast of Madison Square Garden," the crown jewel of the boxing world.

The fight itself was almost anticlimactic. Jeffries had not fought professionally in years and after fifteen rounds in the more-than-100-degree heat, fans begged for the fight to be stopped. But the bout had indeed brought to Reno the national attention it so desperately needed.

In 1913 the state took another step forward. The legislature passed the Suffrage Resolution, thanks in no small part to Anne Martin, one of the most influential (and, in some circles, the least popular) women in Nevada. The daughter of a prominent Reno businessman, Martin was not the kind of woman to take "no" for an answer. An early graduate from the University of Nevada-Reno, the holder of an advanced degree in history and the department's first chairperson, Martin became president of the Nevada Equal Franchise Society. Under her adept leadership, members of the organization began a statewide campaign to convince first the legislature, and then Nevada's all-male voting population, that giving women the right to vote wasn't just the *correct* thing to do, it was the *only* thing to do. With a barrage of press releases, speaking tours, parades, and grass roots organizing, they convinced the members of the legislature to give their wives, sisters, mothers, and daughters their rightful place in the political process. In 1914 the measure was approved by the voters.

*THE LAST WAGON TRAIN. When motorized vehicles failed, the last wagon train to traverse Nevada set out to carry the materials needed to build the highly political transcontinental telephone line in 1913. Photo courtesy of Nevada Bell*

That same year another event convinced the majority of residents that Reno was truly about to enter another era of prosperity. The transcontinental telephone line was completed. Up to that time, the Nevada portion of the line had never been constructed. The people of Reno were linked with San Francisco; why, thought many, did they need to call anywhere else? But at the urging of President Wilson, who was looking for a way to make an international political statement at the upcoming Panama-Pacific Exposition, a new company (Nevada Bell) was formed to undertake the project. Though the desert mandated that the effort be completed primarily by mule and manpower, the trucks bearing Oregon-made telephone poles roared through Reno as crowds cheered wildly. Finally, the city was about to link up with the rest of the world.

While the Truckee Meadows seemed to be on a roll, other areas were feeling the pinch brought about by the decline of the mining industry. Churchill County legislators, looking for some way to attract additional revenue, brought pressure to bear on Reno and succeeded in wresting the highly coveted Nevada State Fair. In 1915, the fair was moved to Fallon. Although Reno politicians made considerable noise over the matter (the newspaper claimed "Fallon Slams Reno Over Fair Matter!") they were unsuccessful. The fair would remain in Fallon until the Second World War.

Though few realized it at the time, just around the corner was a drawing card destined to pump renewed vigor into the city's optimistic but languishing economy. Reno, Nevada, was about to become known as the "Divorce Capital of the World."

*THE LINE'S COMPLETE! The transcontinental telephone line, which was constructed to publicize President Woodrow Wilson's Panama-Pacific Exposition, was completed in 1914. This photo was taken near the site of present-day Wendover. Photo courtesy of Nevada Bell*

*"NEW" POST OFFICE. This "new" post office, built at the turn of the century, functioned until its present replacement was completed on Virginia Street in the 1930s. Photo courtesy of Jean C. Hubbard*

*THE PRIDE OF MACKAY STADIUM. As this elaborate field house attests, football was a prominent sport on the campus of the University of Nevada-Reno as early as 1912. Photo courtesy of Jean C. Hubbard*

BOASTFUL PICTURE POSTCARD. This postcard mailed from Reno (around 1910) illustrates the community's newly emerging pride. The Virginia Street Bridge and the new Masonic Building are prominently displayed. Courtesy of Edwin Bender

STILL THE ONLY WAY TO TRAVEL. Even with the coming of the horseless carriage and the iron horse, the stagecoach was still in active use as late as 1915 (this picture was taken as the horses rested in Dog Valley). Photo courtesy of Ross Wainwright

*FILL 'ER UP! Although there doesn't seem to be much activity, Reno's first gas station (located at 344 N. Sierra) did a booming business. Photo courtesy of Ross Wainwright*

*A FESTIVE VIRGINIA STREET. This postcard looks north on Virginia Street around 1910. Note the frock coat on the gambler in the foreground. Courtesy of Frances Brisbin*

*A PARADE OF ELEPHANTS. Bertha the elephant, present-day mascot of John Ascuaga's Nugget in Sparks, has nothing on early Reno. Here, elephants in East Indian finery strut their stuff in a Circus Day Celebration on Virginia Street in 1911. Photo courtesy of Edwin Bender*

*THE UNIVERSITY EXPANDS. The new Mackay School of Mines, on the University of Nevada-Reno campus of 1912, boasts an underground sprinkler system. Photo courtesy of Edwin Bender*

*POWERFUL AND PATRIOTIC.*
*Although it didn't turn out quite like this,*
*the Reno City Hall was featured promi-*
*nently in early Reno's pride and publicity*
*in 1912. Courtesy of Edwin Bender*

# CHAPTER 7

# The Politics Of The Situation

As the twentieth century dawned, Reno was still struggling valiantly to maintain its identity. Despite faltering attempts to establish itself as a manufacturing and agricultural center, the city remained little more than a wide spot on the now faltering highway of commerce.

The gravity of the situation was evidenced by daily headlines. "How long must this evil be endured?" queried the *Daily Nevada State Journal* on January 14, 1902. "The idle and criminal vagrants of First Street should all be banished from the town!" Continued the newspaper, "Reno is facing a crisis. The citizens of the town have at last awakened to the realization that this city is branded throughout the coast as a wide open town, where vice is uncontrolled and crime stalks rampant."

Into this shaky arena would come two men whose futures would be forever intertwined, two men destined to hold the future of Reno and indeed Nevada in their iron hands for more than four tumultuous decades.

Pat McCarran, Nevada's first native-born senator, was born in Reno on August 8, 1876. George Wingfield, indisputably the city's richest man, was born just eight days later. Both would make their reputations in the mining camp of Tonopah, McCarran as a rash young attorney, Wingfield as a gifted financier. Though they would become bitter enemies, throughout most of their lives they would live within a half-block of each other. Ironically, in death they lie even closer—both are buried in Mountain View Cemetery.

McCarran, astutely aware that the political hub of the state was not Reno, but the mining camps, moved to Tonopah after an unsuccessful attempt to run for the state senate. There he began to establish a reputation as the "champion of the underdog," a position to which he would tenaciously cling throughout his entire career.

One of his earliest cases proved his uncanny ability to grab the limelight. "Popular Sheriff Murdered!" screamed the headlines. The *Tonopah Sun* reported that Manhattan's Tom Logan, one of the state's premier lawmen, had been shot by gambler Walt Barieau. In a move that stunned many, McCarran chose to defend the

itinerant card shark.

His defense was nothing less than brilliant. He set out to discredit the popular sheriff, a family man and father of eight who was said to have at one time faced down the famous Wyatt Earp and lived to tell about it.

It mattered little to McCarran. He brought in witnesses to testify that county funds, while not actually misappropriated, had been "mishandled." He paraded call girls before the jury who testified that Logan, far from being the family man as the prosecution contended, was actually having an affair with one of the girls. He depicted Barieau as an innocent bystander, a man in the wrong place at the wrong time.

The ruse worked. On July 14, 1906, the jury brought in its verdict. Gambler Barieau was found not guilty of the murder. McCarran's future was established.

George Wingfield had arrived in Tonopah a little earlier. Armed with a grubstake from Winnemucca banker George Nixon (who would win a seat in the United States Senate in 1905), Wingfield invested in gambling, mining, and banking. Their partnership would prove golden. Together the two men created the Tonopah Banking Corporation. By 1906 they had opened a bank in Reno, the Reno National Bank; the following year they had established yet another financial institution in Goldfield.

Money seemed to flow magically to Wingfield. With help from none other than Bernard Baruch, he managed to form the Goldfield Consolidated Mines Company at the height of the city's mining boom. The institution had assets of fifty million dollars—an unheard-of amount at the time. When Senator Nixon died in 1912, Wingfield garnered complete control.

McCarran and Wingfield locked horns from the beginning. McCarran had represented Wingfield's wife, May, in a divorce suit and although he lost, he earned the banker's lasting animosity by entering testimony that claimed George Wingfield had forced his wife to have marital relations with him "when he had syphilis."

Their later battles would extend far beyond the courtroom. In 1907 a labor strike threatened the Wingfield empire when miners refused to accept their pay in scrip, a

Washoe Co. Court House.

A SYMBOL OF LAW AND ORDER. The
Washoe County Courthouse was so
impressive that it graced this popular
postcard in 1915. Courtesy of
Frances Brisbin

POWERFUL PAT. Popular United States
Senator Pat McCarran, an opponent of
George Wingfield, addresses an early
political rally. Photo courtesy of the Nevada
Historical Society

*ROYALTY IN RENO. The Nixon Mansion, which still dominates present-day California Avenue, was owned by a California senator who was a business partner of George Wingfield. Nixon held his prominent office from 1905 until 1911. This early photo was taken around 1912. Photo courtesy of Edwin Bender*

move necessitated by the financial panic brought about by the San Francisco earthquake.

Wingfield appealed to his friend, Governor John Sparks, who, along with his old ally Nixon, petitioned President Roosevelt to bring in federal troops. Soon miners were facing heavily armed militia. McCarran, always sympathetic to the underdog, spoke out publicly against the action.

Although a federal commission eventually conceded that Wingfield tricked the president and ruled that "We do find no evidence that any condition then existed not easily controlled by the local authorities," the Wingfield-dominated mine owners were able to break the back of the workers' union, even going so far as to reduce the existing pay by one dollar a day. There was little doubt that George Wingfield had become a figure to be reckoned with.

The boom was coming to an end in the mining camps. In another ironic twist of fate, both McCarran and Wingfield moved back to Reno the very same year (1909). Although Nevada law prohibited branch banking, Wingfield continued to open other financial houses and before long the newspapers were referring openly to the illegality of the situation as the "Wingfield chain." And for good reason. As author Jerome Edwards reports, "By 1932, the Wingfield banks controlled 59.9 percent of the total assets and liabilities of all banks in the state, a dominance unparalleled" anywhere else in the country.

Wingfield's interests branched out immediately. He snapped up extensive real estate holdings in the city, including the two largest hotels, the Riverside and the Golden. Author Edwards mentioned: "It was rumored that he controlled the bootlegging and gambling interests in the wide-open city, in conjunction with Jim McKay and Bill Graham."

It was more than idle rumor. John Sanford, editor of the *Reno Evening Gazette*, stated,

Every little thing that went on around here, everybody said, "Well, now, how's that gonna get along with the boys up there in the cave?" By that they meant the upstairs of the old Reno National Bank building. In one political campaign those who opposed the Wingfield machine used to bring up the war cry of "4111 in Nevada Politics." That was the telephone number. And 4111 gave you the Reno National Bank, George Wingfield, George Thatcher, and Bill Woodburn. George Thatcher at that time—let's see, I believe he was Democratic national committeeman, Bill Woodburn was state chairman and George

OPULENCE. This photo, taken in 1912, shows the famous Riverside Hotel. Note the open-air porch where visitors could enjoy the beauty of the Truckee River or simply watch passers-by. The domed building in the background to the left is the new Reno Courthouse under construction. Photo courtesy of Jean C. Hubbard

Wingfield was national committeeman for the Republicans. So you can see what "4111" meant. And every one of the state conventions that was held around here, Republican or Democrat, the influence of that machine was there.

This web definitely crossed party lines. Among Republicans, Tasker Oddie (governor 1911-14, senator 1921-33), Lester Summerfield, Fred Balzar (governor 1927-34), and Morley Griswold (lieutenant governor, 1927-34, governor 1934) were close to Wingfield. Among Democrats, Key Pittman (senator 1913-40), William Woodburn, George Thatcher, Sam Pickett, Ray Baker, George A. Bartlett and James Scrugham (governor, 1923-26) had ties with Wingfield as well.

But while Wingfield was building the city's most powerful political organization, Pat McCarran was well on his way to becoming the city's most promising attorney. His trademark was emotion; opponents would later admiringly admit that he charmed, rather than persuaded, his juries.

Reporter Sanford recalled one such case:

Pat was at his very best. He was involved with a half-caste Chinese gal from down the line who'd stuck a knife in her boyfriend, and Pat came in there as attorney for the defense. I guess he was just out of practice and wanted to get into his dramatics again. He did! He went on to claim, oh, this poor little beaten down lotus flower of the Orient, who'd been raised in a convent, and so on and so forth, and now, who knows, but if she comes out from under this blush, she may return to the friendly shadow of the convent, and so on. Oh, talk about tear jerkers! He was the very best. Well, it worked. The jury acquitted her. And that night, so they tell me, she did not go back to the shelter of the convent. They held the damndest party there was in town there in one of them old time "houses."

Pat McCarran continued to parlay his ability and soon became a Supreme Court justice. Although he seemed to lack much interest in his new position (he would later

write, "There is no place on earth that constitutes so fine a political burying ground as the bench") he still managed to stay in the thick of all things political, even some that were humorous.

Key Pittman, Nevada's junior senator, had a well-known drinking problem. As such, he was constantly making headlines, and in 1914 he was involved in a fistfight on the streets of Reno. There, listed among the participants, was Pat McCarran.

United States Senator Key Pittman was felled and sent prone in the gutter on Virginia Street yesterday after he made an unprovoked attack on Lytton Stoddard. The scene which occurred in full view of scores of persons on the street at 11 o'clock in the morning, was the culmination of a series of affrays, precipitated by Pittman. The aggregate results follow:
    Struck Zeb Ray, democratic politician
    Struck United States Marshal A. B. Gray
    Struck Senator William F. Sharon
    Struck Supreme Court Justice
        P. A. McCarran
    Struck Deputy Sheriff Lee Updike
    Struck H. Fraley, Republican leader
    Struck Lytton Stoddard
    Struck Virginia Street

Despite their hatred, both McCarran and Wingfield did agree on one issue—prohibition. McCarran, always the crusader for the little man, realized that "the Act" was practically unenforceable, particularly here in frontier Nevada. Wingfield, on the other hand, saw prohibition as a regulation that threatened some of his more nefarious business interests.

Nevada's U.S. attorney, Harry Atkinson, who owed his federal appointment to the banker and whose spacious office was located next to Wingfield in the Reno Bank Building, had this to say, "Prominent people owned bootlegging places. Wingfield might have owned the Reno Social Club. He might have been the undercover, but there was Bill Graham and Jim McKay on the outside. They owned a lot of places during prohibition."

Enforcement by local authorities was nonexistent. Continued Atkinson, "it was hard to enforce prohibition, awfully hard. I told the fellows that we wouldn't stack against anybody. We wouldn't do any underhanded work to catch them or break in or anything like that."

Other G-men from outside the state, however, were considerably more conscientious. "Some of the fellows coming in from the outside were those prohibition agents that you couldn't control, hardly. They were a little bit fast about doing things. They tried to catch me, too. Oh you bet your life! And they tried to get Wingfield because I think his cook or someone like that gave some records to them, or was alleged to have done it. They used a search warrant to search his house. They tried to get the goods on him, but they didn't. Prohibition was a bad 'noble experiment.'"

It was not surprising that most Nevadans looked the other way. Reno itself was now not only populated, but run by, men who had known each other intimately during the boom days in Tonopah and Goldfield. They knew where the bodies were buried. Therefore, it was easy for Wingfield, whose banks had financial influence on almost every public figure and who even controlled the *Nevada*

*State Journal* due to a massive loan to its editor, to completely command the politics of Reno. Licenses and permits were issued, not by the city, but by a call to the infamous "4111." The Wingfield group even managed to keep Pat McCarran from a seat in the U.S. Senate, a position he had been vying for for years.

Still, the secret dealings and the devil-may-care atmosphere allowed Reno to become a divorce capital. It was a decision that would save the city from possible extinction and bring it instead worldwide notoriety.

*TWILIGHT ON THE TRUCKEE. This setting, with its magnificent home on the south bank of the Truckee River in 1915, was worthy of a picture postcard. Courtesy of Frances Brisbin*

*RIVERSIDE DRIVE. This postcard view of Riverside Drive (circa 1915) shows the lack of development in this secluded area along the Truckee River. Courtesy of Frances Brisbin*

*McKINLEY PARK SCHOOL. A visitor pauses before the McKinley Park School in this early Reno winter scene. The prominent flag was later added by a graphic artist. Postcard courtesy of Frances Brisbin*

Virginia St. Bridge, Y. M. C. A. Bldg. and Post Office.

GOVERNMENT AND YOUNG MEN.
*The downtown Reno post office (left) and
the Young Men's Christian Association
share this property along the Virginia
Street Bridge (circa 1915). Postcard
courtesy of Frances Brisbin*

MEN IN MEDICINE. *The all-male
medical staff of St. Mary's Medical Center
in 1912. Photo courtesy of St. Mary's
Regional Medical Center*

*A NEWCOMER. For this picture of a newborn baby, the nurses at St. Mary's pay strict attention. Photo courtesy of St. Mary's Regional Medical Center*

POWER IN POLITICS. *This political rally, as evidenced by the banner across Virginia Street, promotes the Socialist Party ticket of Eugene V. Debs. In 1912, his vice-presidential running mate was Emil Seidel. Photo courtesy of Edwin Bender*

*HOME FROM THE WAR. Nevada soldiers in uniform parade across the Virginia Street Bridge. Photo courtesy of Edwin Bender*

*ZEROLENE OR GASOLINE? At the corner of Fourth and Sierra streets, this state-of-the-art gasoline delivery truck was photographed in 1915. Photo courtesy of Ross Wainwright*

THE CURE. As this cartoon illustrated, Reno had "the cure" for marital problems. Church groups across the country called for political action to end the "outrageous conduct" of Reno, Nevada. Courtesy of the Nevada Historical Society

# Divorce: The Savior Of The City

**D**ivorce came quietly to Reno. And it came from far away.

It was born in the law offices of a New York attorney by the name of W. H. Schnitzer who felt stymied by the length of time required for legal divorces. He soon learned that Nevada, a state with one of the smallest populations, had a waiting period of just six months, an unheard-of period for the times.

Schnitzer immediately capitalized on the situation. He took out ads in the major New York papers, the theater programs, and other periodicals, and soon business was booming. He even provided a free pamphlet that extolled the ease of divorce way out in the romantic wild, wild, west. Requests for further information rolled in. Schnitzer quickly set up legal contacts in Reno who would coin the colorful phrase "quickie" divorce.

Reno's decision to publicize what the state had offered quietly for years was simply a sound business decision. Social mores at the time still limited many divorces to those rich enough to withstand the public persecution, and Nevada's laws offered the city the opportunity for its own upper class, though only on a temporary basis.

One of the first to take advantage of the situation was Laura Corey, an attractive showgirl who made headlines when she arrived in 1906 to shed the president of the powerful U.S. Steel. Soon a rush was on.

The rules were amazingly simple. One had only to live in the area for six months—no slipping over the mountains to spend even a day in California, no side trips for shopping in Salt Lake City. You came to Reno and you stayed. Period. Still, as rustic as the city was in the early part of the century, for the hundreds of wealthy people looking to shed their spouses, it was well worth it.

Newspapers across the country were incensed. The clergy preached hell and damnation from the pulpit. The city was likened to Sodom and Gomorrah. But when names like Vanderbilt and Astor began to appear on the scene, most of the residents, while engaging in arresting gossip, simply looked the other way.

Locals seemed to bask in the national attention. After all, many reasoned, if the rich could get a divorce without

burning in the fires of Hades, why not the common man and woman?

The town rolled out the red carpet. To help make things even more painless, Reno attorneys, normally highly competitive, created a standard divorce fee of just three hundred dollars. Cab drivers rattled off the names of law offices as easily as they did the names of the most prominent hotels.

Business leaders touted the ease of a "Reno Divorce," citing examples of men who were granted separations on charges no more solid than "I find her beauty fading." Women could claim they had "a man with wanderlust" and the results were typically the same.

Yet a small, but vocal, minority still put up a fight. A group of Reno housewives mounted a moral crusade, even going so far as to hire a train. They crammed the cars to overflowing with irate women and descended en masse on the Carson City legislature. Instead of a six-month waiting period, they advocated an increase to one year. Their crusade worked. The legislature, bending to this well-orchestrated outcry, increased the mandatory length of stay.

But the accomplishment would cost the business community dearly. Wrote Max Miller, "Towns soon became ghost towns. The stores in Reno gave up their luxury lines. Show windows which once contained furs and silks for the New York trade began showing overalls and simple frocks again. Even the women who had launched the crusade suffered. Ironically, many of their own husbands are now out of a job."

Then, as now, the legislature met every two years—a fact that suddenly became disastrously apparent to merchants in the city. It would not be until 1915 that the legislature convened again, and once in session they wasted no time in changing the law right back again. This time the political pressure was powerful and male. Wrote Miller, "'Oh, he's one of the guys who voted for 12 months' was a phrase sufficient to damn any political aspirant." Miller was right. Not a single member of the legislature who voted for the law was ever again re-elected.

When the furor had subsided, the city began a period of steady growth. Guesthouses on the outskirts of town

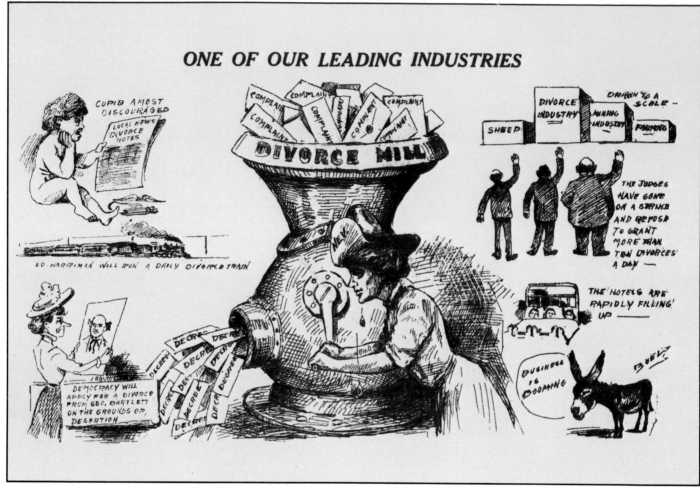

*A NEW BUT DISTURBING "INDUS-TRY." This early cartoon trumpeted the popularity of a Nevada, and more particu-larly, Reno divorce. "The hotels are filling up rapidly." Courtesy of the Nevada Historical Society*

were spruced up in preparation for the many who came to take advantage of the once again liberal divorce situation.

Still, the press was not entirely convinced of the wisdom of such liberty. It didn't help that visiting reporters looked down their noses at Reno. Wrote author Katherine Geroald in 1925, "How do people bear the boredom of living here for the six months necessary to get a divorce? There is horse racing and it attracts a large crowd. Never has a race track had a lovelier setting, but the races last only 21 days out of the year. What do they do with the rest of their time?"

She went on to suggest that if she herself were waiting for a divorce a drive in the country might be nice, but she hardly felt like driving alone. She mentioned the possibility of a trip to Lake Tahoe but warned against the urge, for Tahoe was too close to California and "divorcees should not be caught so close to the temptation of freedom."

"There are no plays in Reno, no music, no galleries, and hardly even a library. Women who reside in Reno for 6 months of waiting are thrown absolutely on their own resources for 6 months in a strange land." She solved the problem in later pages of her book by suggesting that one possible solution for those plagued with a Reno stay would be to take a lover.

In the twenties, thirties, and forties, the names of those who came to town would make a serious contribution to a list of the nation's rich and famous. There was Mary Pickford, the most popular star of the silent screen, who liked the area so much that she built a permanent home on Arlington Avenue. The star was sagely represented by none other than Pat McCarran.

There were Constance Bennet and Liz Whitney, Orson Welles, and even a wealthy Indian maharaja. While some took advantage of the gambling and twenty-four-hour-a-day, free-flowing alcohol, most were content just to pass the time. Bennet regularly went duck hunting. Mary Pickford, sporting the clothing favored by ranching wives, quietly went about her business at a Minden guesthouse.

*THE HUB OF COMMERCE. The Reno Mercantile Company on the corner of Sierra Street (shown here in 1917) later became the Hagerman and Schooling Store. Photo courtesy of the Nevada Historical Society*

*SPARKS IN 1922. The view (east) along Sparks' business district shows the horseless carriage sharing the main thoroughfare with the iron horse. Photo courtesy of the Nevada Historical Society*

*EVERY TIME THE CLOCK TICKS, WE PAY A DIME TO SOMEBODY! The Skeels-McIntosh Drug Store dominated the corner of Virginia and Second streets in 1921. Note the insurance advertisement near the top of the building. Photo courtesy of the Nevada Historical Society*

*APTLY NAMED. The Wigwam Theater attracted full houses during the early years of silent pictures. Photo courtesy of the Reno Orthopedic Clinic*

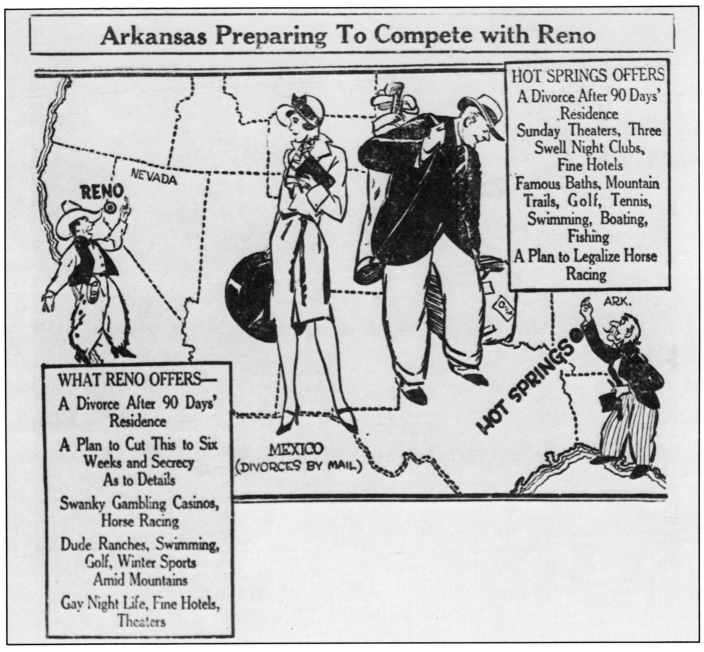

## Arkansas Preparing To Compete with Reno

**HOT SPRINGS OFFERS**
A Divorce After 90 Days' Residence
Sunday Theaters, Three Swell Night Clubs, Fine Hotels
Famous Baths, Mountain Trails, Golf, Tennis, Swimming, Boating, Fishing
A Plan to Legalize Horse Racing

**WHAT RENO OFFERS—**
A Divorce After 90 Days' Residence
A Plan to Cut This to Six Weeks and Secrecy As to Details
Swanky Gambling Casinos, Horse Racing
Dude Ranches, Swimming, Golf, Winter Sports Amid Mountains
Gay Night Life, Fine Hotels, Theaters

NEVADA • RENO

MEXICO (DIVORCES BY MAIL)

HOT SPRINGS • ARK.

*"WHAT RENO OFFERS..." The competition for the divorce trade was heating up. This early survey proclaimed that while Reno offered a "gay night life" and fine hotels and theaters, Hot Springs, Arkansas, had "Swell Night Clubs" and a plan to legalize horse racing. Courtesy of the Nevada Historical Society*

With the passing of years, however, not all of the furor had disappeared. A Reno bishop in 1923 began complaining publicly to reporters from the *Nevada State Journal* that it was outrageous for a town to attract visitors with sin. Members of the local chamber of commerce immediately called a special session. They managed to convince the bishop to, as the paper stated, "put a stop to his foolishness." After all, business was business.

Was the divorce law really that good for the little town on the Truckee? In truth, yes. Writer Miller, who visited Reno during the height of the divorce era, wrote

scathingly: "If Nevada adopted the New York divorce laws, overnight, in less than 6 months, Reno would be about as alive and prosperous as Tonopah. The University of Nevada would still sit on its hill, but there would be very few shops and garages left and I fancy more than one bank would fail."

Writer Geroald summed up the feelings of much of the populace:

Even the convinced and honest Nevadan must admit that a good many of the divorces are not

*THE UNIVERSITY COMES INTO ITS OWN. By the time that this postcard went on sale around 1915, the entrance to the University of Nevada-Reno campus just off Center Street was a popular gathering place. Courtesy of Frances Brisbin*

*WINTER SERENITY AT UNIVERSITY OF NEVADA-RENO. Snow blankets Manzanita Hall at UNR in 1912. Photo courtesy of Edwin Bender*

*PICTURE PERFECT. This unidentified University of Nevada-Reno student pauses in front of the Mackay Building in 1912. Photo courtesy of Edwin Bender*

morally pretty and are acquired without due regard to personal responsibilities and other people's rights. But I think that he will always cling to his conviction that it was better to have laws abused than to abolish them.

Nevadans do not worry over abuses as much as an easterner, simply because he is used to minding his own business. East of the Missouri no one minds his own business, but west of the river people really do mind it.

I do not mean to hold up the sovereign state of Nevada as an example of legal purism. Nor is it an especially law-abiding state. It is wild country, most of it, pretty well unredeemed to civilization. Perhaps the only laws that they respect are laws that give, not curtail freedom. They more or less ride steeplechases through the rest I fear....

Reno's flamboyant mayor, E. E. Roberts, was typically in the thick of things. Roberts, who had previously won a bid for Congress by advocating "getting rid of the Chinese," was no less outspoken about a Reno divorce. The mayor actively campaigned on the slogan—"A whiskey

barrel and a dipper on every corner." He was quoted as saying, "It's all nonsense to try and regulate people's morals. I don't believe in any kind of reform which takes away from any man or woman the right to find happiness in their own way. I would repeal all blue laws and make Reno the playground of the world!"

For a time it seemed to the rest of the nation that Reno, Nevada, was truly "sin city," still a place of cowboys and wild Indians, but now also of degradation and corruption. In the 1930s a movie called *Charlie Chan In Reno* epitomized the negative publicity of the divorce era. In an opening scene in which Chan is being driven south on Virginia Street, the cab driver turns to his passenger and says, "You know, Mr. Chan, just about the only reason people ever come to Reno is to get a divorce."

Unbeknownst to many, Reno would soon be in the limelight again. For several years a move had been afoot to legalize, once and for all, something that Nevadans had also tolerated for years—gambling. The movement would alarm the entire nation. Attempts would be made to recall Nevada's statehood.

*A TYPICAL (?) STREET SCENE. This early postcard, which was popular around 1915, depicts early Reno as the land of cowboys and, especially, Indians. Courtesy of Frances Brisbin*

*HORSE, OR HORSELESS? Even in the early 1920s, the suburbs of Reno were difficult to traverse. Photo courtesy of the Nevada Historical Society*

*FULL SERVICE. This early Reno gas station offered a full range of car care service. It was located on the corner of West First and Stevenson streets in 1920. Photo courtesy of Ross Wainwright*

*ANYTHING HAULED ANYWHERE. As this 1920 photo attests, the moving business in the area was brisk. These two businesses were located on B Street in Sparks. Photo courtesy of Ross Wainwright*

*WINGFIELD HEADQUARTERS. From his offices on the second floor of the Reno National Bank, George Wingfield dominated Reno politics for an entire* *generation. The building, at Virginia and Second, remains little changed from when this picture was taken around 1915. Photo courtesy of the Nevada Historical Society*

# The Dawn Of The Gambling Age

**R**ECALL NEVADA'S STATEHOOD!" was the glaring headline in giant script across the front page of the *Chicago Tribune*. Nevada had just done the unthinkable. It had legalized gambling, and most of the nation wasn't very happy about it.

Church groups predicted hell and damnation for the citizens of Reno, the state's largest city. Politicians across the country ranted and raved about the "deprivations of a backward state." If the stories coming out of the East were to be believed, Reno, Nevada, was going hurriedly to hell in a handbasket.

Actually, Governor Fred Balzar had signed not one landmark bill into law that fateful day, March 20, 1931, but two. One formally legalized the gambling that had been going on for decades, and the second reduced even further the state's divorce requirements, lowering them—much to the chagrin of a startled nation—from three months to six weeks. But the divorce bill was lost in the shuffle of damning publicity that swept the country. The rest of the nation was up in arms about legal gambling. The city of Reno, thought many, was nothing more than a modern-day Sodom with the added convenience of electric light.

There was never any real question that gambling would eventually be legalized. Despite the outcry by many of the citizens, the incredible influence brought to bear by Reno's politicians virtually assured passage. John M. Townley, in the preface to his book *Tough Little Town on the Truckee*, wrote of the city's politics: "Well mannered debate before crowded town meetings never solved public questions, but rather money, influence and the direct purchase of votes. Despite a virtual 100% turnout of eligible male voters, a closed elite determined policy and officeholders. Occasional altruists emerged, but those rare innocents rarely inconvenienced either party."

From "the cave" (his offices in the Reno National Bank Building), George Wingfield continued to wield power supreme. Wingfield, although a Republican, was able to control the Democratic machine as well through his legal associates Bill Woodburn and George Thatcher. The Democratic powerhouse conveniently maintained offices right next door.

Still, the city itself seemed unconcerned. Although gambling had been "legal" on and off for more than sixty years, the community and not the industry had been there first. Local residents, though divided on whether gambling would bolster the economy, were quite blasé.

To understand the indecision of the populace, the reader must note that the period between the two world wars, though one of confusion, would forever set the stage for the growth of the city. On the one hand was the genuine desire to bring Reno into the twentieth century, to improve its image and the quality of life by restricting the vices which up to this point were considered an integral part, if not a right, of the frontier. On the other hand was Reno's longing for commercial success that had so far eluded the city in the shadow of the mining booms.

The line that divided the two was difficult to measure. It was true that the resources available in the immediate vicinity were, with the exception of mining, severely limited. The valiant, though futile, attempts by Francis Newlands to create an agricultural center of the city had failed. What did the region really have to offer? It boasted mining, ranching, and real estate—the latter consisting of hotels, gambling halls, and saloons. Wingfield fought, indeed schemed, to protect these industries from any form of restrictive regulation.

Reform was needed, it was true. But would reform discourage investment, growth, and the money-making attitude of "devil-may-care"? Reno was a city plagued by insecurity that was easily swayed by those who favored uncontrolled expansion.

The mayor was for it and spoke out in no uncertain terms. Said the mercurial E. E. Roberts, "For the past 8 years, I've been trying to make Reno a place where everybody can do what they please, just as long as they don't interfere with other people's rights. Now we can do lawfully what Nevada has always done undercover!"

The controversial gambling bill had been introduced in a roundabout way by Phil Tobin, a cowhand from Winnemucca. Although officially proposed in the legislature by another man, at the last moment Tobin was asked to put his name on it when the embarrassed

*THE NIXON BUILDING. The horse and buggy had all but disappeared from Virginia Street by the time the K. I. Nixon building was completed. Photo courtesy of Edwin Bender*

politician began to feel the pressure from his spouse.

Tobin, however, felt no such reluctance. "I had no love for gambling or gamblers," he said. "It's just that I didn't think it could be done away with and the state was almost broke. After all, we were in the middle of a depression. I just wanted to see gambling pay its own way. Some of the tinhorn cops in Reno were collecting 50 bucks a month for allowing it. Back then, $50.00 could feed a whole family for an entire month."

Actually gambling had been legal in Nevada since the days of the first silver booms, but in 1910, having decided that it attracted an "unscrupulous crowd," the state succumbed.

Quite naturally, making it illegal didn't stop anyone. Gambling merely went underground, as was the case during prohibition. To get into a Reno gambling hall (hall, perhaps, is too strong a word—most gambling places were still little more than hole-in-the-wall operations) all one had to do was be "a local."

On the outskirts of Reno, proper gambling actually enjoyed a tremendous degree of respectability. If Reno was Sodom, vice kings James "the Cinch" McKay and Bill Graham made a nightclub called the Willows Camelot. The Willows featured free-flowing whiskey and a wide assortment of illegal table games. The idle rich, such as the Duponts and the Whitneys (in Reno for the "cure"), didn't see anything wrong with having a little clandestine fun at the same time.

But all that changed officially in 1931. "Gaming, Divorce Bills Signed," said the *Nevada State Journal*. "Preparations are underway to attract sporting crowds. Travel and publicity freedom are lures for divorce seekers."

Other towns, however, were opposed to the new law,

*FROM MINER TO BANKER. Power broker George Wingfield inspects an ore sample in 1927. In the minds of many, Wingfield controlled the city's future. Photo courtesy of the Nevada Historical Society*

*LINDBERGH COMES TO RENO.
Famous aviator Charles Lindbergh spoke
in Idlewild Park in an effort to gain
support for airport improvements. Photo
courtesy of the Nevada Historical Society*

and they were vocal about it. Wrote the editor of the *Carson Daily Appeal*, "The passing of the 6 weeks divorce law and the gambling law is nothing to be proud of. Both measures could have been forgotten and the state would have been better off from a moral standpoint."

In the thick of things was Reno's mayor.

Roberts had led a most colorful life. He had come to Nevada before the turn of the century to watch the Corbett-Fitzsimmons fight in Carson City and decided to stay. After a stint as district attorney, he ran for the U.S. Congress and, with the help of such powerful friends as George Wingfield, he won handily, campaigning on a platform that was blatantly anti-Chinese and—more important to the pro-growth faction—pro-irrigation.

In Washington, he made the headlines regularly. The first time was on the occasion of his marriage to the daughter of Walter "Big Train" Johnson, the ace pitcher of the Washington Senators and the closest thing to a national hero at the time.

Roberts consistently spoke out against the United States' involvement in the First World War. "Better for us and those who come after us that we never entered this war," he roared. "If it is traitorous to oppose what will lead to the establishment of a despotic military system, then I plead guilty to the charge!"

His stand against the war, however, was not as popular here as at home. One evening at the Riverside Hotel, he was confronted by an angry businessman who

*FLAMBOYANT MAYOR. Mayor E. E. Roberts poses with his all-male city council in the 1920s. The mayor, described by many as "a dandy," campaigned on a slogan of "a whiskey barrel and a dipper on every corner!" Photo courtesy of the Nevada Historical Society*

accused the congressman of being unpatriotic. In typical short-tempered fashion, Roberts promptly knocked the accuser to the floor.

Upon his return from Washington, Roberts, now armed with more than a few influential friends from his days in the capital, began to rebuild his law practice. He would specialize in divorce over the ensuing years, claiming to have handled more than two thousand cases and losing only one. Said Roberts about that client, "He was a chump. He lied to me. He didn't tell me that he had another wife. I didn't find out about it until she showed up in court."

It was 1923 when Roberts first set his sights on the mayor's office. The city boasted more than fifteen thousand citizens, and the main issue, not surprisingly, was prostitution. The winds of reform, fanned by World

War I, had caused statewide attacks on the trade from Ely to Las Vegas. Roberts, knowing full well that some of his own political backers were themselves involved in running prostitution rings (though a city ordinance had closed the town's Red Light District), was still unwilling to confront such powerful groups as the League of Women Voters, the Monday Club, the Reno Women's Temperance Union, and the Women's Faculty Club.

With savvy that would become his trademark, Roberts chose a campaign strategy: prostitution would not disappear, but if elected, he would guarantee to confine it to the eastern part of town. He was elected by an overwhelming margin and, true to his word, the new mayor established Reno's infamous Stockade—a depressing assortment of low buildings consisting of more than fifty "cribs" and accented by a small club called the Pastime.

Throughout his tenure in office Roberts was always in the limelight. He hosted Charles Lindbergh at Idlewild Park when the hero arrived to promote the new concept of national airmail service.

He was praised for his beautification efforts, but was condemned by the press when it was learned that ten of the new policemen assigned to his city parks program turned out to be personal friends.

His ability to garner the limelight won him a second term as mayor in 1927. Roberts oversaw the Transcontinental Highway Exposition which was jointly sponsored by Nevada and California to celebrate the completion of U.S. Route 40—the new Victory Highway, and the Lincoln Highway. The celebration allowed Roberts to reap the rewards of growth and expansion while improving the city at the same time. Newly dedicated Idlewild Park became the primary site of the exposition, and the state of California built the California Building on the grounds, donating it magnanimously to the state of Nevada. For the first time, the national press announced that the forbidding "Great American Desert," which formerly was looked upon as something to be avoided when vacationing, was now easily accessible. An arch was erected spanning Virginia Street, indicative of the city's new sense of accomplishment. Growth and progressive expansion had triumphed over reform—the shuttle service to the Golden Hotel was called a "charming improvement." That same year, the Reno Rodeo ("Reno's Annual Carnival of the Range!") touted $5,000 in prize money.

In 1930 Roberts decided to run for governor. But when he was defeated by Fred Balzar, Roberts, undaunted, ran again for mayor. Again, he succeeded. His popularity, although conspicuously lacking in the press, was nonetheless evident in his personal relations with reporters. He often invited his favorites to hunt with him on his ranch at Spanish Springs. He began his day with a shot of whiskey mixed with milk. "It is the secret of my robust health," he declared.

Insiders, however, scoffed that it was not a championing of personal rights, but his own penchant for alcohol that comprised much of the mayor's platform; this theory seems to be borne out by some of his more quotable outbursts. He spoke to the congregation of the First Methodist Church to defend his position on the subject. Soon there were headlines proclaiming, "Mayor in pulpit declares free liquor would solve evils!"

John Cahlan, a reporter for the *Reno Journal*, recalled at the time, "If there ever was a politician that looked like a politician, it was Roberts. He always walked down the street in a big frock coat, with cane and derby hat, with a big gold chain draped prominently across his vest. Because derbys weren't popular in Reno at the time, he was quite a sight. A real dandy!"

It was in this atmosphere that the city, with a "dandy" for a mayor, found itself with the passage of the gambling and divorce bills. Dr. Clarence True Wilson, national director of the Methodist Board of Temperance, called Reno "a combination of Sodom, Gomorrah and perdition."

"Gambling is bad business, anyway you look at it," said Roberts—again utilizing his uncanny ability to walk a tightrope. "But it is far more desirable when it's conducted out in the open and not behind closed doors." On the subject of the new six-week divorce, Roberts offered, "If a person is going to get a divorce, they are going to get it one way or another. We want them to get it here. It's good for all of us."

E. E. Roberts would die in 1933, shortly before his sixty-fourth birthday. But he had seen his landmark bills pass. The epitaph that lingers, however, did not appear on his tombstone. Of Roberts, reporter John Sanford wrote: "He was a pretty good ol' scoundrel in his way."

And as the city entered another turbulent era, Reno, Nevada, thought many, was indeed run by scoundrels.

CRUISING UNDER THE 1938 ARCH.
*This photo shows that the center of commerce had finally shifted from Commercial Row to Virginia Street. Note the pennants draped across the busy thoroughfare. Photo courtesy of Harvey M. Moll*

# CHAPTER 10

# The Turbulent Thirties: A City Torn

"Reno is a blot on civilization, a menace to the
American home and national prestige."
*The International Society of Christian Endeavor*

Nevada's new laws, legitimizing gambling and creating the new month-and-a-half waiting period for divorce, had much of the nation up in arms. Not surprisingly, most of the attention was focused on Reno, the state's largest city. Just a few short years before, on the occasion of the Transcontinental Highways Exposition, Reno had brazenly begun calling itself "The Biggest Little City in the World!"

The city had more to worry about than its image as a "blot on civilization." The town was suffering from the effects of a record drought in 1930 and 1931 which devastated ranches and crop yields throughout the state. To make matters worse, a crippling depression was gripping the nation and Reno was about to be crippled as well.

It is no wonder then that residents preferred to look the other way when negative publicity surfaced. "Reno makes its living, as far as one can tell, off the marital unhappiness that prevails in 47 other states of the Union," wrote Katherine Geroald. "The divorcees bring a certain amount of money into the place, and banks, shops and markets are kept going in that way. The churches are inconspicuous; the few doctors have Chinese herbalists for hot rivals; the lawyers, naturally are many."

Geroald continued, "The public library is so tiny that it could not possibly keep anyone in reading matter for 6 months, and if there were a run on its shelves, most of the besiegers would have to stop in the street."

She was, however, not quite so critical of the city's courthouse. Wrote the author with no small degree of cynicism: "The Washoe County Court House is a handsome building and quite large enough to accommodate any number of simultaneous divorces."

Those "simultaneous" divorces had a name. They were being called, interestingly enough, "Renovation"—a term coined by popular newspaper columnist Walter Winchell. (Ironically, in the 1960s, the city, led by downtown business interests, would begin a cleanup process that would bear the same name).

Still, most of the publicity failed to mention the fact that many people were coming to Reno not for a divorce, but to be married; as always, it was the state of California which had unwittingly bolstered the city's economy. In 1927 in an attempt to encourage the sanctity of marriage, California had passed the so-called "3-Day Gin Marriage Law" which required a three-day waiting period in the hopes that, given time to think seriously about the consequences of matrimony, more bad matches would be prevented.

The legislation, however, only spurred an increase in Reno's tourist economy. Anxious newlyweds simply drove over the mountain to a place where they could be married, not in days but in minutes. To this day, many of Reno's wedding chapels owe their very existence to this virtuous legislation.

And if locals merely shrugged off the hullabaloo

surrounding the new divorce law, they likewise looked the other way at the vice that was controlling the city.

Wrote James Rowley in his *Reno, the Hub of Washoe County*:

> In 1934 FORTUNE magazine referred to the five who ruled Reno. They included Wingfield, Woodburn, Thatcher, McKay and Graham. McKay and Graham owned the Cal-Neva Lodge at North Lake Tahoe, the Willows Roadhouse west of Reno, and had investments in many other establishments, including the Reno Social Club in partnership with Wingfield. Their businesses involved the risks of running liquor from the Bay Area across state lines. They occasionally harbored big-time criminals—Baby Face Nelson, Ma Barker and perhaps Alvin Karpis—from the Midwest in their Reno dives and laundered money and securities received from outside connections.

The allegations were true. As the third decade of the century dawned, Reno was known as "the big store"—in gangster parlance, it was the place to launder money. It was well known that Graham and McKay, for a small fee, would assist the criminal element in trading in any ill-gotten gains through their gambling halls.

It took the FBI to bring an end to Reno's infamous duo. In 1934 federal charges were brought against Graham and McKay and they were eventually convicted on charges of mail fraud, although not without another scandal. Scheduled to testify against the pair was Roy Frisch, a cashier at the Riverside Bank, which, like the hotel, was owned by none other than George Wingfield. Frisch was last seen walking up Court Street. He simply disappeared and his body was never found. Rumor circulated that Baby Face Nelson had "returned a favor" for his two benefactors and dropped the annoying Frisch down the nearest deserted mine shaft, but it was never proven.

It was in the autumn of 1932 that the most devastating blow was unceremoniously dropped upon the state and its "Biggest Little City." For some time, the state's primary banking operation, the Wingfield chain, had been suffering some serious setbacks. The fall of the stock market on Black Monday in 1929, compounded by the drought of the following year, had placed the twelve Wingfield banks in serious jeopardy. The situation brought about what anti-Wingfield forces had been trying to accomplish without success for years.

George Wingfield, through perhaps loose accounting practices and his own opposition to state regulations, found himself overextended. Earlier, in desperation, his banks had received a $4 million loan from the RFC (the Federal Reconstruction Finance Corporation). Additional loans were obtained from the Federal Reserve Bank in San Francisco and the Crocker First National Bank. The loans would prove painfully inadequate.

Panicked, Wingfield applied for additional funds from the RFC, even enlisting the aid of Governor Fred Balzar who flew immediately to Washington to meet with none other than President Herbert Hoover. Although the

president and representatives of the Reconstruction Finance Corporation were polite, they refused to advance additional funds due to Wingfield's now-apparent lack of collateral.

The ominous predictions of long-time foe Pat McCarran had finally come true. In later years, McCarran, now a senator, would write to his daughter, "On the 31st day of October, the Wingfield chain of banks closed their doors. The closing of the Wingfield banks destroyed the financial and industrial life of the State of Nevada."

He outlined the true effects of the impact, most of which were yet to be felt:

> In addition to this, the Wingfield banks, by reason of political affiliation, and by reason of political power had in their custody some one million, two hundred thousand dollars of public funds. They crippled every form of life. School moneys were involved. The funds of the University were tied up. The funds of the schools of every district were tied up and the funds belonging to the State Treasury were tied up—so that State employees were unable to receive their monthly salaries.

The impact of the crisis trickled down to even the smallest shops and stores in Reno's business district. Continued McCarran:

> The business life of the State was the recipient of [a blow to] the solar plexus. Immediately following this, the San Francisco wholesalers issued an order that no credit would be extended for the shipment of goods to the merchants of Nevada. Cash must be on hand before shipments are made, hence the credit extended by retailers was immediately curtailed—in fact, destroyed entirely.

McCarran was not exaggerating in the least. It was no wonder that the residents of Reno had more to worry about than their reputation as "sin city." The entire foundation of the state's financial base had been shaken to the core.

As the senator philosophized in later years:

> The reason is that too much power was vested in one individual and whenever too much power is vested in one human being, that power usually turns in the form of a flame—to destroy the political, financial and moral power of the State— as for the last 15 years has been vested in George Wingfield. He was an avaricious controller, demanding the pound of flesh in every line in which he bent his efforts. The God of nature seems to destroy such a condition, and it has come here. It is the greatest blessing that has come to this commonwealth in 20 years.

McCarran's rage against the man whose influence had kept him from the halls of the United States Congress finally surfaced. "The power that controlled the throttle of

*AD AGENCY ON WHEELS. Your message could be carried from "Reno to Los Angeles" in 1930. Note the sign for Edises Jewelers, a firm which still exists. Photo courtesy of the Reno Orthopedic Clinic*

Reno's Hotel Golden is the largest in the state and one of the most colorful. It is the meeting place of old timers in the Nevada cattle and sheep ranching empires, and mining engineers from all corners of the 315 mining districts in Nevada. It's lobbies ring with high heeled boots, jingle with spurs. No big hats here . . . this is not dude territory but the real thing. Legend says the hotel was once won in a poker game. Tradition says many a state law, many a candidates' fate was settled in informal legislative caucus here. Fact says it is a large, air conditioned, modern hotel . . . usually well filled.

*"NOT DUDE TERRITORY." This late 1930s postcard continued the Reno gambling image. It alluded to the possibility that the Hotel Golden had been won in a poker game. Courtesy of Bennett Photos*

*RENO'S FAMOUS BANK CLUB. Early lighting techniques highlighted the Bank Club on the corner of Center Street and Douglas Alley. Photo courtesy of Neal Cobb*

this state is at an end, and although the people may go back to the throes of impoverishment, they nevertheless will reap the benefit in many ways. It is a blessing of purification."

It would take years for most residents to agree. The Depression continued, and even though America had a new president, Franklin D. Roosevelt, who spoke prophetically that good times were just ahead, few in Reno were believers.

Even the legalization of gambling that many thought would take up the slack and bring renewed prosperity to the city had little impact. Most of the gambling houses— with names like the Bank Club, the Rex Club, and the Wine House—were still dark and smoky places within the confines of Douglas Alley. Along Center Street, establishments with such unlikely names as the Dog House, the Inferno, the Northern, the New Yorker, and the Bonanza held forth. Their patrons were all male, and cheerless males they were.

Thankfully for Reno, Nevada, there were a few people like Raymond I. "Pappy" Smith just around the corner.

*RENO GENERAL. This 1930s photo shows the Reno General Hospital, located at Ralston and University Terrace. At the time, it looked more like a home than a hospital. Photo courtesy of St. Mary's Regional Medical Center*

*A FABULOUS FOURTH. This 1938 picture suggests that the entire city turned out for a traditional Fourth of July parade on Sierra Street. Spectators were encouraged to wear a carnation in their lapel. Photo courtesy of Harvey M. Moll*

GAMING COMES ALIVE. Reno's growing dependence on gambling was evidenced by these entrants in the 1947 Rodeo Parade. They are dressed entirely in playing cards. Photo courtesy of Neal Cobb

CHAPTER

11

# Gambling Comes Of Age

If the biggest problems of 1933 were the Great Depression, the failure of the Wingfield banks, and the earlier Nevada range drought, there was still one small glimmer of hope. "U.S. PROHIBITION IS REPEALED!" screamed the *Nevada State Journal* on December 8.

Among the stories on the front page was the claim by a New Yorker that he had somehow managed to buy the country's first truly legal drink of whiskey. Renoites, however, were hardly interested in such frivolity. After all, they had been drinking "somewhat" legally for years.

The new Roosevelt administration's policies, created to provide jobs and to get America "back on the track again," affected Reno to a sizeable degree. Under such programs as the CWA, PWA, and the WPA, both Mackay Stadium at the University of Nevada-Reno and Virginia Lake Park in the southern portion of the city were constructed. Senator Pat McCarran was on hand when the new swimming pool in Idlewild Park was dedicated. Construction costs, half of which were paid by the federal government, reached close to $150,000.

Fortunately, the city of Reno was not quite as helpless as the rest of the nation. As the New Deal era approached, most metropolitan areas were forced to increase taxes—in some cases, in dramatic proportions. To counteract the negative response to higher taxation, these same areas quite naturally took great pains to increase their public services as well, using government funds to build new and better roads, irrigation projects, and educational facilities.

Reno, however (as did the state of Nevada) shunned both. On the state level, Norman Biltz advocated that Nevada's only chance of emerging unscathed from the Depression was to keep taxation low, thereby attracting the wealthy to invest. As a result of his efforts, his proposal—dubbed "One Sound State"—initiated caps on property tax rates and prohibited estate and inheritance taxes. While other states were searching frantically for ways to tax the rich, Nevada was, as usual, doing exactly the opposite.

Nevada welcomed the well-to-do with open arms. In 1935 Max Fleishmann brought his wealth to Glenbrook,

which benefited the entire state immensely. The philanthropist stated candidly, "A millionaire doesn't deserve a damn bit of praise for using whatever money he has to help other people, but he deserves a lot of discredit if he doesn't." Fleishmann's fortune would fund part of the state museum, numerous clinics, libraries, parks, and pools, and provide $25 million in grants to the university system.

Locally, thanks primarily to legal gambling, Reno appeared to be relatively healthy. Although the gaming industry had yet to truly come into its own, most of the revenues collected from gambling taxes were not shared with the state but rather kept, for the most part, by the local government. This convenient arrangement relieved to a substantial degree much of the burden felt by other cities at the time.

Gambling was not yet a significant draw for the city, and for good reason. There was still enough of a stigma connected with it that tourists, with the exception of usually rowdy servicemen, were not exactly pouring over the hill to partake.

Perhaps even more important was the lack of the more serious gamblers, those able to lay one thousand dollars or more on the table. "The true gambler," wrote Max Miller, "is not at his best as an artist playing with thousand dollar bills at the same green table with a schoolteacher-on-vacation, a sheepherder, a bookkeeper, and a convention delegate playing with dimes—and they doing all the screaming at every turn. We can see why such time-tried artists as Nick the Greek considers Reno gambling nothing at all—nickel stuff for those who cannot afford it, meaning nickel stuff for those who at heart are not gamblers though they may imagine themselves to be."

Miller was quite accurate in his descriptions. The visitors of the thirties found several clubs of any size, such as the Bank Club and the Palace. Places like the Tavern, the Town House, Leon and Eddie's, and even the venerable Riverside Hotel were known for their drinks and camaraderie rather than casino play. Such establishments as the Dog House, the Ship and Bottle, and the Inferno were more renowned for their floor shows. Most local Basques played quietly at the Northern, and the Club

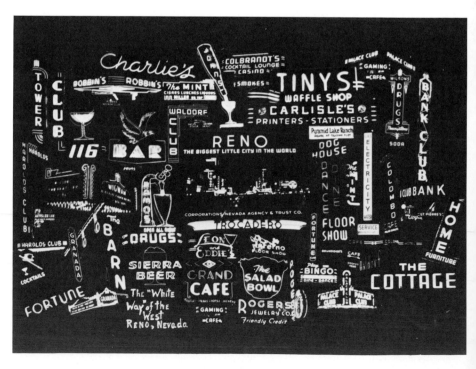

*RENO IN 1941. R. Herz Jewelers and the Nevada Club still remain today. Note Bill Harrah's Bingo sign on the left side of the street. Photo courtesy of Neal Cobb*

*SIGNS OF THE TIMES. This collage of Reno business signs was created by a local photographer in the 1940s. Courtesy of Bennett Photos*

RENO GOES COSMOPOLITAN. This 1942 postcard suggests that the Riverside was located "virtually in the center of Reno." Note the cars parked on the Virginia Street bridge. Courtesy of Bennett Photos

Fortune touted itself (less-than-proudly) as a "bingo salon."

"Reno gambling," said Miller, "despite its wide-openness, is anything but gilded. It is, in fact, downright tawdry—almost as tawdry in spirit as a public beach resort which goes in for winning hams, dolls and frying pans."

Enter the Smith family.

Ironically, they came from the very same type of background as that mentioned by Miller, the carnival and bingo circuit. But the Smiths had bigger things in mind.

At age twenty-six, Harold Smith opened a small operation that seemed destined for greatness from the start. A flamboyant promoter weaned on the "smell of the crowd," Smith Jr. had the carny instinct. But it was the shrewd business sense of Harold's father, Raymond I. "Pappy" Smith, that lent sound business practices to the fledgling business. Pappy minded the money while Harold added a new, yet essential ingredient—color—which

would set the stage for most casino growth through the forties and fifties.

Harold Smith, by his own admission, was one of Reno's biggest gamblers. (In his book *I Want To Quit Winners*, he confessed to losing more than a million dollars of his own money.) He brought much of the carnival with him to the city. An avid horseman, he frequently rode his horses right into the casino, Harold's Club, much to the delight of patrons who, up to now, thought those kinds of things happened only in the movies.

The Smiths were the first to apply publicity "gimmicks" to the gambling industry, and throughout the subsequent years some were successful, some were not. No matter, they all seemed to make the news.

One of their earliest roulette games featured caged white mice. Though cute and cuddly, they did little for the speed or profitability of the game. Later, during one of

*FROM THE TOP OF THE RIVERSIDE. In 1945, the roof of the Riverside Hotel afforded a great view of a metropolitan Virginia Street. Photo courtesy of Neal Cobb*

many expansions, Harold built a waterfall of real whiskey. It was discontinued quickly when workers and patrons complained that the fumes literally intoxicated them.

The Smiths even created a portable horse-betting window. Unwilling to sacrifice lucrative floor space on a permanent horse-betting window, Harold's Club engineers created one mounted on an elevator. When horse racing was over for the day, the betting window would descend into the basement where workmen removed the window, replaced it with a craps table, and sent the new game back up into the casino.

The owners of other gambling halls laughed, calling Harold's Club "Smith's Honky-Tonk" and the "Gambler's Five-and-Ten." But Smith was unfazed. He was convinced that if gamblers were given a chance to play in surroundings that were exciting and colorful, they would return the favor by calling Harold's Club home. His reasoning was sound.

The Smiths bet their fortune on two distinctly different, but as yet unheard-of, commandments. The first was a sign that hung prominently outside the office of Raymond I. Smith. It read, "No One Can Win All the Time. Harold's Club Advises You to Risk Only What You Can Afford." To owners of the other gambling halls, the concept bordered on heresy, but customers loved it. It helped that Smith's door was always open, even to his players. Underneath the previous sign was another that said, "Push on the doorknob to beat hell!"

The second premise fostered by the growing casino was the phrase—"It Takes Winners to Get Players"—and the casino was careful to practice what it preached. In 1947 two University of Chicago students arrived in Reno with a toy roulette wheel and began keeping meticulous records (in gamblers' terms, "clocking the wheel"). While many seasoned veterans laughed, Al Hibbs and Roy Walford began to run up winnings that at one point totalled more

ON THE HOUSE. *The ever-present and ever-popular host, Raymond I. "Pappy" Smith, pours one for a customer in 1944. Though Smith was scoffed at by local gambling interests, his flair for publicity-making made him a Nevada legend. Photo courtesy of Neal Cobb*

GAMBLING COMES OUT INTO THE DAYLIGHT. *By 1947 gambling had moved from Commercial Row and Douglas Alley to Virginia Street. Photo courtesy of Bennett Photos*

*THE NEW CHINA CLUB. By the early 1960s, entrepreneur Bill Fong had given blacks and orientals their own casino. During the 1940s and into the early fifties,* *even popular entertainers such as Sammy Davis (who appeared with the Will Mastin Trio) had to use a side entrance. Photo courtesy of the Nevada Historical Society*

than $13,000. So enraptured was the city by their progress that daily bulletins could be heard on the radio, and the pair even appeared in *Life* magazine. Instead of discouraging such outlandish play, as many casinos at the time would have done, Raymond Smith chortled happily to the *San Francisco Chronicle* that you "couldn't buy the publicity for $150,000."

It was the Smith family who, for the first time, actively began to advertise casino gambling outside the state, and veteran advertising executive Tom Wilson created a masterful campaign. Wilson, who some years before had stimulated publicity of the "Reno divorce" by purchasing cheap imitation diamond rings at Woolworths and then flinging them into the Truckee (thereby lending credence to the myth that divorcees threw their weddings rings into the river), was now convinced that casinos could and, indeed, should advertise their own unique brand of "Nevada style fun!"

Wilson contracted with more than forty radio stations in the West, and his concept provided a general theme upon which Harold's would capitalize for decades. The

commercials made no mention of actual gambling. They described instead the beauty of Nevada, particularly Lake Tahoe and the Sierra, proclaiming that the region was "a year-round playground." Wilson and the Smiths were betting that once the vacationer was nearby, he or she would be unable to resist the urge to visit their casino. It was a masterful stroke. Soon the establishment was being touted as "the world's largest." Suddenly size and the uniqueness of the action were drawing cards every bit as effective as gambling itself.

Their famous ad campaign—"Harold's Club or Bust"—made headlines across the country, and even as far away as Europe and Asia. Wisely realizing that servicemen travel, Harold's made available small signs and sent them free (along with a few complimentary decks of playing cards) to members of the armed forces. Willingly the soldiers carried these miniature billboards to the four corners of the globe. Reno was prominently mentioned on all the signage, and soon Reno and Harold's were synonymous. Better still, they were famous.

There were good and bad points to the relationship.

On the one hand, when the Jim Beam Distillery came to town to create a special decanter for Harold's, $10,000 worth was sold within forty-eight hours and another boxcar load had to be shipped in. Upon arrival, cars lined up behind the delivery vans, and people flew from all over the country to get their hands on a sample of true Americana.

On the other side of the coin, however, such publicity bred more than its share of crime. Responding to a tip that Harold Smith, Jr., was about to be kidnapped, Reno police hurried to the scene. They discovered only an innocent-looking flatbed truck piled high with lumber. But when one of the investigators leaned against one of the boards, a trap door opened. Inside the stacked lumber was a large room, apparently the proposed hiding place for the victim. The alleged kidnappers managed to escape.

Hot on the heels of the Smith family came another entrepreneur, William Fisk Harrah, who opened the Tango Club in Douglas Alley a year later in 1937. Initially unsuccessful, Harrah moved his operation onto Virginia Street in 1939 and from there he never looked back. Today, although the Harrah family is no longer connected with the operation that bears his name, it is the largest gaming organization in the United States.

To say that the two casinos single-handedly set the tone for the gambling era that was yet to come is by no means a falsity. While the Smiths were flamboyant, almost wondrously childlike in their approach to gambling, Bill Harrah took the concept and upgraded it to include unparalleled quality. From the carpeting, to the fixtures, to the genuine leather upholstery, Harrah would build a reputation that could only be described as "class." There was room for both in the growing metropolis.

The traditions that the Smiths and Harrah established proved monumental in terms of name recognition, not only for themselves, but for Reno as well. This is evidenced by the fact that, though the men are gone, their names still twinkle with lights.

Ironically, both organizations had much in common for competitors. They were both actively involved in setting up scholarship programs for the university, and both created sizeable, though secondary, legacies that remain to this day. The Harold's Club Gun Collection, purchased from historian Bill Stagg for $35,000 for the opening of their Roaring Camp display in 1949, remains one of the finest collections of Old West memorabilia available. Bill Harrah's love of classic automobiles has grown into the most prestigious and famous assortment of vintage cars in the entire world.

But there were others who were instrumental in setting the rules and direction of the industry over the years. There was John Petrecciani who began with just two "21" tables and who, along with Warren Nelson, re-established the highly profitable oriental game of Keno after managing to convince state officials that it was not, despite its legal definition, a lottery.

Lincoln Fitzgerald brought recognition of another kind. In 1949 the owner of the tiny Nevada Club was "cut down" by shotgun fire as he walked along the sidewalk near his home. Fitzgerald never pressed charges for the attempted assassination and never openly discussed the matter. Still, it was rumored that organized crime, which had previously been limited to Las Vegas, had finally come to Reno. Robert Laxalt quotes an "insider" on the event: "Fitz was just a gambler. He was never in the rackets. But the boys had done him a favor when he was in Detroit. When he set up shop in Reno and made a go of it, they decided to collect their due bill. They wanted in. Fitz said he wanted to stay clean. They wouldn't accept that and that's why he got it." Fitzgerald in later years apparently was no longer fearful of his life. He went on to build a new hotel that bore his name. In a then-unheard-of move, perhaps reminiscent of his association with organized crime, he paid cash for the entire construction project.

And there were others. There was Bill Fong, who took over the old Palm Saloon and, after extensive remodeling, reopened the place under the name of the New China Club, which offered blacks and orientals the first place they could truly call their own.

Of course, there was Jessie Beck, who parlayed her meager beginnings with the Harrah organization into a hotel-casino of her own.

There were more, of course, hundreds of them—men and women who were bigger than life, capable of generating their own myths and legends. But perhaps more importantly, they were astute business people in the right place at the right time. Reno, Nevada was definitely the right place. Soon, the time would be right as well.

As the 1930s came to a close, few doubted that the phrase the "War to End All Wars" had been a misnomer. Europe was engulfed in a fiery confrontation, and most Renoites believed that it would only be a matter of time before the United States joined in.

Throughout the Southwest, training areas were springing up. Servicemen, anxious for a little excitement, rolled into Reno for a chance to get in on the action.

When the war began, the friendly face of Reno's gambling industry began to change. Women dealers appeared on the scene for the first time, and the universally patriotic moniker "Rosie the Riveter" took on new meaning in the gambling halls of the Truckee Meadows. With "Rosie" behind the tables, more and more women began to venture into establishments that formerly had been off limits except to those of questionable virtue.

It was now the gambling interests that controlled the city, just as the Wingfield machine had ruled in years past.

There were those who refused to copy the example set by the Harold's Club billboards, fearing that public sentiment could again outlaw an industry that was just beginning to grow. Just the same, the casinos were banding together for common protection.

A classic example of gaming versus government occurred in 1940. Federal agents were about to close the off-track betting parlours throughout the city. The raids, which were considered merely another outrageous encroachment by big government, were well publicized; the date of the proposed action was not. It mattered little. When District Attorney Ernest Brown prepared a confidential memo which would be given to members of the legislature on the proposed morning of the shutdowns, a copy was immediately leaked to Bill Nash, a popular athlete and announcer at KOH (the state's only radio station). Nash read the memo in its entirety over his news broadcast, alerting everyone to the impending raids and effectively destroying any further attempt to close the city's race books.

But until the Second World War, despite the efforts of the Smiths and Harrah, the vast majority of Reno clubs were little more than carnival booths, casual and totally localized.

All of that was beginning to change. Gambling in Reno was coming of age.

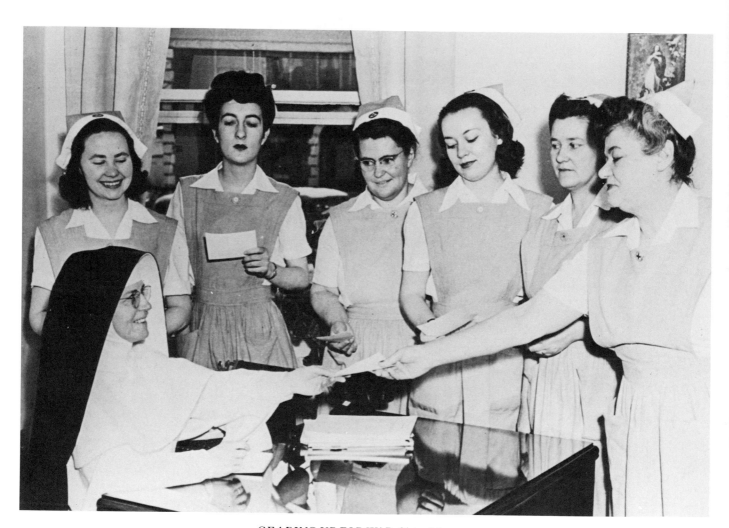

*GEARING UP FOR WAR. Sister Mary Seraphine accepts donations from Red Cross nurses' aides. Photo courtesy of St. Mary's Regional Medical Center*

*A WORLD PREMIERE! Although the Errol Flynn movie bore little resemblance to the true history of Virginia City, promoters arranged a "world premiere." Photo courtesy of the Harry O'Brien Family*

*THE SPIRIT OF SPARKS. Sparks war bond sales financed the purchase of this WWII bomber. Photo courtesy of the Sparks Heritage Foundation and Museum*

*THE BOYS IN BLUE. Reno motorcycle officers Carl Broberg (left) and Bob Eberling pause for a photo in front of Parker's Western Wear, a Reno landmark since the forties. Although most police vehicles had had radios since the late 1930s, calls to police were received through KOH, Reno's lone radio station. When emergency calls came in, the KOH broadcast was interrupted. Prior to the period, street patrols used lights strategically placed on tops of buildings to alert officers to call in. Photo courtesy of Neal Cobb*

*THE GREAT EQUALIZER. This "Hoover for President" truck, used for a Jeannie Crane movie filmed at UNR, roamed the streets of Reno in the mid-1940s. Photo courtesy of the Harry O'Brien Family*

106

*FIRE! Firemen try in vain to reach the roof of the Odd Fellows Building in this 1945 debacle. Photo courtesy of Neal Cobb*

*CHRISTMAS ON THE RIVER. In 1945 the Truckee River became a festival of lights over the Christmas holidays. Photo courtesy of Bennett Photos*

THE BLIZZARD. This man does not appear to be making any headway against the raging blizzard conditions that seemed to plague the city during the 1940s. Photo courtesy of Bennett Photos

A GREAT RESORT. At Reno Hot Springs, located at the intersection of Mount Rose and Highway 395, locals and visitors alike could enjoy the city's largest swimming pool. Photo courtesy of Neal Cobb

*ON THE WAY TO CARSON. Passengers wait to board the famous V & T at the Reno station in 1945. Photo courtesy of Neal Cobb*

*STRIKE UP THE BAND! Back in 1947, Reno's Municipal Band was attracting music lovers to the steps of the State Building. Today the band, sans uniforms, still continues to perform. Photo courtesy of Neal Cobb*

*NOW THAT'S A "BIG" HAT! A popular restaurant with locals, the Big Hat was located on the corner of South Virginia and Moana Lane. Even in the 1940s the restaurant stayed open until 4 a.m. Photo (circa 1949) courtesy of Neal Cobb*

*ALL ABOARD! A costumed judge passes out promotional materials to the crew of the Virginia and Truckee prior to a sightseeing trip to Carson City in 1945. Photo courtesy of Neal Cobb*

*THE AIR AGE FINALLY ARRIVES. This aerial view of the Reno Municipal Airport (circa 1945) shows a United DC-3 at the gate. To the left is the main ticket station. Photo courtesy of the Greater Reno-Sparks Chamber of Commerce*

*BANKING IN 1952. The First National Bank Building at First and North Virginia Streets. Photo courtesy of Bennett Photos*

# The City Comes Of Age

Locals bristle when they hear people say that "Reno is a backward town, behind the times." But it's true. It has been true for decades.

By the end of World War II, as the rest of the nation was getting back to normal, Reno and the state were still trying to become respectable by making some changes that, though turbulent, were long overdue. Most Americans remember the late forties and early fifties as a carefree time, but for the citizens of Reno it was a period when the city would undergo such dramatic changes that it would never be the same again.

With V-J Day came a great deal of uncertainty. Reno's hopes of becoming a center of commerce had failed to materialize during the war years, and gambling had become increasingly more popular. If the city was to build on its infant reputation as a tourist mecca, a clean-up was in order.

Pressure from the federal government had been brought to bear on Reno's infamous Stockade (home of the "cribs") as early as 1942 when servicemen were warned to "stay clear." By the close of the war, prostitution in Washoe County had been declared a "public nuisance." As the decade came to a close, the courts upheld the rights of a county to regulate the morals of the people; business interests, now convinced that proximity to the "world's oldest profession" was hurting tourism, acquiesced.

While much of the old city was disappearing, the downtown area was taking on a new, more modern appearance. In 1947 the Mapes family announced that they would build a new luxury hotel right at the river's edge ("It will be Nevada's tallest building!"). In terms of being new and different, it was not an idle boast. Its revolutionary Sky Room played host to such luminaries as John Wayne, Johnny Weismuller, Liberace, Harpo Marx, and Beatrice Kay. Noting with glee that huge crowds were now hitting the streets after late shows at the Mapes, other casino owners hastily added graveyard shifts, even in the middle of winter.

During that same year, the city council created Reno's Red Line Ordinance, restricting casino gambling primarily to the Virginia Street area.

The region surrounding the city was growing as well. Ski resorts, formerly the playground of the wealthy during the divorce era, had now been discovered by the average American. Suddenly, as Tom Wilson had predicted, Reno had yet another drawing card.

Presidential attention was heaped upon the city. On September 22, 1948, the entire town turned out to honor Harry Truman as he moved through the west on a campaign tour. Truman was treated to a dazzling Virginia Street parade and a ceremony in Powning Park. Realizing he was on safe ground in traditionally Democratic Nevada, the president seized the occasion to jab deftly at the opposing party. He quipped, "They are just a bunch of old mossbacks!"

*A NEW AGE FOR RENO. In 1947 the Mapes hotel was nearing completion. When it opened in November of that year, it was Nevada's tallest and perhaps most luxurious building. Photo courtesy of Neal Cobb*

*WIDE OPEN SPACES. This aerial view of the Veteran's Administration Medical Center at Locust and Kern shows little development in the area. Photo courtesy of Bennett Photos*

*CHAIRLIFTS TO THE SKY! By the mid-1950s, skiing had become a popular attraction for tourists. Note the banner promoting the nearby slopes and the marquee touting a risque French revue. Photo courtesy of Bennett Photos*

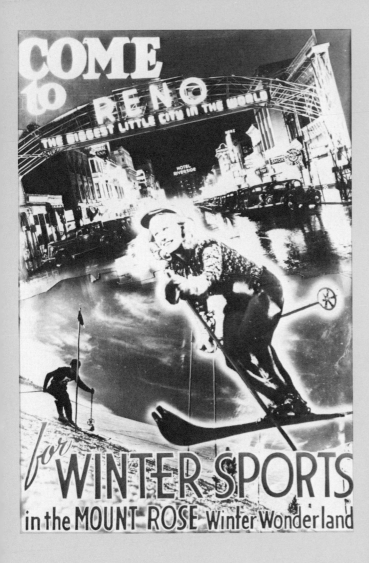

WINTER SPORTS IN RENO. This 1940s poster was part of a growing effort to attract tourists to Reno by emphasizing the growing popularity of winter sports. Courtesy of Bennett Photos

STOMPING THE SAGEBRUSH. At a quiet moment on his tour through Reno, President Harry Truman is presented with a portrait as a memento of the occasion. Photo courtesy of the Greater Reno-Sparks Chamber of Commerce

At the state level, more changes were taking place. Realizing that the gambling industry was here to stay and that the state was missing out on an increasing amount of revenue, the legislature in 1945 levied a 1 percent tax on the gross receipts of Nevada's casinos. By 1947, they doubled it to 2 percent, then added an additional "table tax."

The men in charge of regulating Nevada's still amateur industry were the members of the Nevada Tax Commission, a group of unpaid but powerful business leaders who represented a wide range of economic sectors—mining, land, livestock, and agriculture. Though skilled in these other fields, the members of the commission learned soon enough that to police the

gambling industry would be no easy task.

By the time the commission had increased its staff and become more knowledgeable about the industry over which they had gained control, the federal government stepped in. Senator Estes Kefauver made the first of many trips to the Silver State to investigate what were being touted as Nevada's "ties with the country's hoodlum element." Shortly thereafter, a bill was introduced in the United States House of Representatives to lay a federal tax on Nevada's casinos. Only through the energetic, often behind-the-scenes efforts of powerful Senator Pat McCarran was the measure defeated.

Of the impact of such a bill McCarran said, "Virginia

*BENDER THE WAREHOUSEMAN. Frank Bender, son of Edwin Bender, posed for this photograph (right) early in his career. Bender was instrumental in creating Nevada's unique regulations which eliminated many of the taxes on goods in storage. Photo courtesy of Frank Bender*

*HOLDING UP THE CEILING. The statue inside the Bonanza Club (left) appears to be holding up the ceiling. These people seem oblivious to the fact that the figure is nude. Notice that some practical joker has placed eyeglasses on the rugged lady. Photo (1945) courtesy of Neal Cobb*

*"TOO INVOLVED FOR THE YOUNGER GENERATION." This postcard (right) which shows the interior of Reno's Bank Club, touts Faro—the "Famous gambling game of the Klondike." Courtesy of Bennett Photos*

Street would be in mourning and the gleaming gulch of Las Vegas would be a glowing symbol of funeral distress." Politically, it was not an easy stance for McCarran to take. "One does not feel very lofty when his feet are resting on the argument that gambling must prevail in the state that he represents. The rest of the world looks upon him with disdain even though every other state in the Union is harboring gambling in one form or another."

Still, the focusing of such national attention served only to illustrate more fully the dependence of the city on gambling. Wrote McCarran, "Nevada's 20th century prosperity did not grow by expanding payrolls of industrial or manufacturing establishments. It was accomplished by making the State of Nevada a playground to which the world was invited, and that playground has as its base gambling in all forms."

Nonetheless, Reno was obviously dependent on the tourist dollar and was judged by many to have a precarious existence at best. Edwin Bender, as a federal administrator in charge of storing strategic materials during the war years, realized immediately the possibilities of Reno becoming a major warehousing center. He set out to buy as much land as possible.

When the war ended, Bender found the situation reversed. Now instead of housing tons of material awaiting shipment to the front, Bender found himself with empty warehouses. When the county tax assessor attempted to levy the same tax on a vacant warehouse as on a full one, Bender rebelled. "It is hard enough," he said, "to get business in Nevada without assessing warehouse storage for tax revenue."

Bender refused to let the matter rest. With the help of

**FARO BANK IN Reno**

Faro Bank, famous gambling game of the Klondike is the choice of old timers in Reno. This complicated game is too involved for the younger generation as a rule. Shown is a Faro game at the Bank Club.

*WELCOME TO THE RODEO. This cowgirl, suspended across the intersection of Virginia and Second streets, touts the Reno Rodeo in this early 1940s picture. Photo courtesy of the Greater Reno-Sparks Chamber of Commerce*

*REAGAN COMES TO RODEO. This rare picture shows Ronald Reagan and Jane Wyman in town for the Reno Rodeo. He was never seen with a cowboy hat. Photo courtesy of the Harry O'Brien Family*

*76 TROMBONES. The Billinghurst
Band strut their stuff on Center Street in
1947. Photo courtesy of Neal Cobb*

another powerful senator, Alan Bible, he drafted what would become known as the Freeport Bill, which stated that goods in storage or transit through the state would be free of tax assessments. In conjunction with the lobbying efforts of the chamber of commerce and local newspapers, and with the assistance of state assemblyman Marvin Humphrey (who was also his nephew), Bender saw his bill become law in 1949. Within ten years, the law would be firmly rooted in the constitution of the state and would become still another attraction for the city.

During the 1940s, Reno's population had increased by more than ten thousand, many of whom had been attracted by the city's image of big money and fast times. Indeed, Nevada's personal income statistics showed that Renoites were enjoying a family income level much higher than the national average. As the 1950s dawned, Reno's hourly wages were among the highest in the country.

Still, there were many questions about the labor practices of Reno, particularly among those engaged in the now-burgeoning tourist industry. Things came to a head over the Independence Day weekend of 1949.

For years a conflict had been brewing between the culinary and bartending workers of the city and the management of many of the resorts. The workers, under the direction of William Royalty of the Bartenders and Culinary Union, prepared to strike for higher wages, and they were confident of the best time to drive home their demands.

Reno's biggest weekend of the year, in terms of the influx of visitors, traditionally was linked to the Fourth of July and Reno's annual rodeo celebration. When the union announced that they would throw up picket lines at this, the time when the town should have been rolling out the red carpet, the entire city was in turmoil. The mayor, Francis Smith, as well as the editorial boards of the city's newspapers, appealed to the workers to postpone their demands until July 6. The union refused.

Hastily, a Citizen's Emergency Committee was formed. As author James Rowley chronicles, "They issued a call to the people of Reno declaring, 'Our vital tourist industry is threatened—you are now asked to help save it in this grave emergency.'"

MICE, NOT DICE. "Pappy" Smith plays the dice game he devised which used live mice. The concept, though it attracted considerable attention and the accompanying publicity, thankfully never became popular. Photo courtesy of the Greater Reno-Sparks Chamber of Commerce

Full-page ads summarized the gravity of the situation. The advertisements begged the citizens to "roll up their sleeves and pitch in as dish washers, cook's helpers, waiters, bartenders, busboys and any number of similar jobs." An alternate plan was announced to feed the thousands of tourists who were expected. Powning and Horseman's Parks were to be thrown open to visitors and food would be laid out in an attempt to provide "the same first class service the Reno visitor has now come to expect."

It was to no avail. On Sunday, July 3, some seven hundred workers went on strike publicly demanding equal pay for male and female employees. Because of the impact of the strike, community leaders and hotel casino management would develop a searing resentment toward those who formerly had been valued friends and employees. Such pressure was brought to bear that, in 1951, Nevada officially became a "Right to Work" state, subject to the approval of the voters the following year. Although the measure passed by a scant one thousand votes, the die was cast—Reno and Nevada remain governed by the law to the present day.

Perhaps the biggest change to affect the city would come in the middle of the decade. The country's first interstate highway law had been introduced by Nevada Senator Tasker Oddie, and by 1956 the National Highway Act was passed. It would have a lasting impact on the "Biggest Little City in the World."

Realizing that Reno was virtually cut off by heavy snows from the state of California (its most frequent supplier of gamblers) during almost one-third of the year, Raymond I. "Pappy" Smith once again demonstrated his far-sightedness. He proposed that a four-lane, all-weather highway be built across Nevada into northern California, replacing the antiquated two-lane Highway 40. Dipping into his own pocket, he manufactured metal signs that read: "Let's make this four lane. Write your congressman."

Enlisting the help of the various chambers of commerce along the way, he succeeded in strategically placing the mini-billboards along the entire proposed route—effectively bombarding the traveling public with continuous messages about the advantages of swifter, more convenient transportation. For those tourists trapped in winter snow or bogged down in bumper-to-bumper traffic, the message was clear. Gamblers, as always anxious to hit the tables, wrote letters by the thousands.

The completion of the all-year highway was the most important event of the decade. Wrote Norman Biltz, "I think it will be as important to Nevada as the building of the railroad in 1867."

Though entering a new age of growth and prosperity, the city of Reno was still a victim of mismanagement and lack of planning, and water, just as it is today, remained a problem.

In the early fifties, a series of disastrous floods inundated the city, and, after much study by the Army Corps of Engineers, their recommendations resulted in the

*A RIVER ON CENTER STREET.*
*Rescuers use rowboats during the raging*
*flood of 1950. Nearly three million dollars*
*in damages would plague area businesses.*
*When the Truckee River reached its peak,*
*some twenty-five thousand feet per second*
*of water poured over its banks. Photo*
*courtesy of Neal Cobb*

*SAFETY IN THE SKY ROOM. The*
*disastrous flood of 1950 could be viewed*
*best from the famous Mapes Skyroom. At*
*street level, as this fallen tree attests,*
*conditions were much worse. Photo*
*courtesy of Neal Cobb*

*SWIM FOR IT. In 1950 flood waters engulfed the Donner Inn Motel and the Flying Star Service Station on Vine Street. Photo courtesy of the Greater Reno-Sparks Chamber of Commerce*

*HERE IT COMES AGAIN! By 1955 the flood waters had come again. Here workers wade through the water which overran the sand bags that had been placed strategically by citizens. As indicated by the stains, the actual water level had dropped almost three feet by the time this picture was taken. Photo courtesy of Nevada Bell*

creation of Stampede Dam and Prosser Reservoir.

But it was the shortage of water, not the abundance, that left many people worried. Many residents warned that the landscape as described in Walter Clark's *City of Trembling Leaves*, published in 1945, would soon be no more. A movement was mounted to install water meters within the city limits.

Educational difficulties were cropping up. Years earlier, educator Earl Wooster had observed the all-too-obvious evidence of an upcoming baby boom while walking down Virginia Street. He warned that the schools throughout the state would soon be in for a rude awakening. Said Governor Russell in addressing the legislature in 1954, "Enrollment in the schools of many counties has been increasing so rapidly during the last several years that collapse of the elementary and high school educational system, due to deficit spending, is a distinct threat."

The solution, as always, was money. In 1951 Nevada's teachers' salaries ranked in the bottom quarter of the national scale and many were holding forth in buildings that were original—some more than sixty years old. That year it was determined that only 10 percent of the state's educators received an annual salary that even approached four thousand dollars.

To combat the situation, a group consisting of several hundred concerned parents and educators met in Reno under the sponsorship of the Parent-Teacher Association. There, legislators warned that the problem could only be

*ON THE CAMPAIGN TRAIL. Popular governor Charles Hinton Russell deplanes in Reno. Russell, who campaigned on a platform to reorganize state government, served from 1951 to 1958, defeating Vail Pittman both times. Photo courtesy of Neal Cobb*

*THE MOVIE SAYS IT ALL. There were colorful skirts everywhere in the mid-fifties. Here members of the Rainbow Girls parade along B Street in Sparks. Photo courtesy of the Sparks Heritage Foundation and Museum*

*THE FAMOUS V & T. The Virginia and Truckee Railroad, which linked Reno, Carson, and Virginia City, ran from the late 1860s until 1950. This late forties photograph was taken shortly before the last run. Photo courtesy of Bennett Photos*

alleviated by a sales or income tax. Local gambling interests declared that they were already shouldering more than their fair share. The group voted overwhelmingly in favor of a state sales tax. By 1952, the organization was openly calling for a 2 percent sales tax statewide.

In Reno things were getting worse. Children were being subjected to split sessions and odd hours. A group of young parents appeared before the Reno School District Board of Trustees in protest. Historian Mary Ellen Glass recalled, "The board's reaction was to provide a quick course in the realities of politics and finance. Advising that relief lay with the state legislature and not with the school district the school board members suggested that the parents approach the governor and the legislature for appropriate action." The suggestion resulted in the formation of the Washoe County Citizens for Public Schools.

In 1955, bending to considerable pressure, the state legislature finally agreed to revise Nevada's tax base; it

had been an uphill battle. Concerned parents, often dubbed "little mothers" in the press, lobbied the members of the legislature almost every day it was in session. Many in the state had been openly divided—claiming either that a sales tax would bankrupt the state or that to broaden the tax base was "appropriately sensible." Still, the lawmakers conceded to the immense public outcry, and the law was passed. Governor Russell, as he had promised, signed it into law.

But the inexperienced, though energetic, proponents had yet another battle ahead. A Las Vegas group, calling itself Volunteers in Politics, immediately circulated a petition asking the voters to reject the new law. Although many of the signatures collected were obvious duplicates and, in some cases, outright forgeries, they received enough backing to bring the matter directly to the voters in 1956.

Again, private citizens and educators joined forces. A group called the State Committee to Retain the Sales Tax was formed, Reno attorney Bert Goldwater at the helm. Educators Alleta Gray and Beverly Linnecke stumped the state by forming campaign committees in all outlying towns. The *Nevada State Journal* followed up with editorials pleading for help.

In the fall election, their efforts were rewarded. The sales tax was retained by an overwhelming margin of almost 70 percent. Reno schools would soon see substantial improvement. Concerned citizens had managed to do what many considered was preposterous: they had voted to tax themselves. Crowed the *Journal*, "They have smothered repeal proponents with logic and common sense."

But while educators were pushing for better school facilities, casino interests continued to push for further expansion. Their most valiant crusader in Washington, Senator Pat McCarran, had died in 1952 and many feared that federal intervention in Reno's gambling would shortly begin again. There was a definite attitude of "make hay while the sun is shining."

And for good reason. Wrote one Las Vegas newspaperman:

With rumbles of federal action aimed at taxing gambling out of existence, Nevada's legal variety have suddenly come to realize that their Big Stick in the nation's capital is gone. And what's more,

McCarran left no friends behind that can be called upon to lend a sympathetic ear. Quite the opposite, Senator Pat ran roughshod over so many of his colleagues that they would welcome the chance to put the hooks to the Nevada gamblers he protected so savagely.

As the decade of the fifties came to a close, Reno had experienced the most sweeping changes in its history. Gambling, as we have come to know it today, had finally arrived. Reno now had a right-to-work economy, and tourism—the city's lifeblood—was being fueled by an all-weather highway. The Freeport Law had been passed, enabling those who refused to submit to the inevitability of gambling as the region's only true industry to experience a glimmer of hope.

By 1959, 40 percent of the people of Nevada lived in Washoe County. Las Vegas had replaced Reno as Nevada's largest city. The state itself had increased its population by 75 percent, capturing the title of the "fastest growing in the union." During that same year, Reno's hourly wages were the highest in the country—$2.67 an hour or 120 percent of the national average.

On the surface it looked like the city was taking on a new direction and a new prosperity was just around the corner.

*BREAKING GROUND AT GREENBRAE. The start of construction on the Greenbrae Shopping Center in Sparks. The project spelled doom for the merchants on B Street (circa 1959). Photo courtesy of the Sparks Heritage Foundation and Museum*

*THE IMAGE OF RENO? The larger-than-life figure beckoned passersby to the Virginia Street entance of the Primadonna in 1976. Photo courtesy of the Greater Reno-Sparks Chamber of Commerce*

# The Race To The Present

The face of Reno during the 1960s would change dramatically.

In the downtown core area, the casino industry had begun to construct hypnotically colorful new facades comprised of millions of twinkling lights. Their doorways, open now to the street twenty-four hours a day and protected by invisible curtains of air, beckoned customers—with the help of a free coupon or two. Gone were all the smoke-filled back rooms.

Bill Harrah, though now tremendously successful, surprisingly enough had to turn to his neighbors at the Riverside and the Mapes whenever he had guests to put up. He set about to remedy the situation. In 1962 the venerable Golden Hotel, once the bastion of life in the downtown area, burned to the ground, and Harrah snapped it up immediately. Others took the cue, and swank hotel towers began to sprout like desert grass from the valley floor. Searchlights, which could be seen from the top of the Sierra, swept the night sky. During the daytime hours, huge balloons bobbed like miniature dirigibles in the ever-changing wind. Locals returning from California would wryly comment that the skyline of the city seemed to be changing almost daily. Some old-timers were openly complaining that the town would never be the same again. Though many threatened to leave, few did.

Another gambling-related phenomenon occurred in 1964—the creation and acceptance of a brand-new currency. Learning that the federal government was about to phase out "Ikes," or silver dollars, Harrah's, without hesitation, approached the Franklin Mint. As collectors swarmed into the city to snap up the remaining Eisenhower dollars, Harrah's placed fifty thousand newly minted coins into play. They were slightly larger and heavier than the Ike, and valueless beyond Nevada borders, but they were warmly welcomed by gamblers and merchants alike. Residents were proud to say, "Good as gold. Just as damn good as the real thing!" Reno, Nevada, was now minting its own money.

The Redline issue (which restricted casino growth to the immediate downtown area) was being hotly contested both publicly and privately. A. M. Smith, of the city's Committee on Gambling Licensing, questioned "whether the original concept was designed by and for the protection of small non-gambler/businessmen or whether it was done by gaming controlled businessmen for the benefit of the gaming industry.

"If a few are able to exert this type of control through 'just and proper' city government, the ultimate of this pressure might well extend beyond the realm of the gaming industry and could influence every service industry associated with gambling," he warned.

*A TOUCH OF CLASS. Bill Harrah, whose style first brought elegance to the Reno gambling establishment, in the 1960s. Photo courtesy of the Nevada Historical Society*

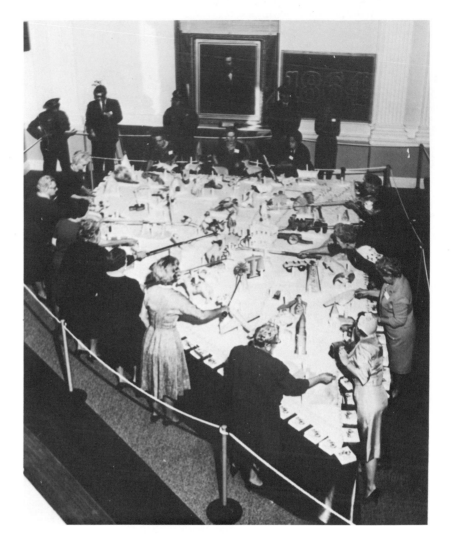

NEVADA'S LARGEST CAKE. *The final touches are added to the state's largest cake in celebration of Nevada's centennial in 1964. Photo courtesy of Mark Savage*

NEVADA CELEBRATES ONE HUNDRED YEARS. *From left to right, actor Ben Alexander (*Dragnet*), Jack Benny, Governor Paul Laxalt, and advertising executive Tom Wilson prepare to cut the centennial cake. Photo courtesy of Mark Savage*

Leon Mandel, in his biography of gaming pioneer Bill Harrah, picks up the story:

Smith insisted that there was a gambling conspiracy he called the "Big Ten" in Reno. He claimed that the Big Ten had bought out "potential troublemakers," that they had succeeded "in loading the local political organization with their men." He insisted that this consortium had "acquired control of over 85% of the property within the Redline." He found this appalling, particularly since he saw no opposition coming from nongambling businessmen in Reno, many of whom were absolutely dependent on supplying goods and services and therefore could not afford to speak up.

Still, there was other growth not so controversial. On the hill overlooking the city, the university was increasing its size dramatically. Having survived several scandals during the previous decade, the emphasis was now on the quality of higher education. A grant from the Fleishmann Foundation had resulted in the construction of new buildings to house the agriculture and home economics departments. The Mackay School of Mines, named for the only Comstock millionaire who kept his money in Nevada, was separated from the engineering department and accredited. A grant from the estate of Wesley Travis resulted in a new student union building. A university news service, with young newsman Robert Laxalt at its head, had been created.

To the south, a prosperous residential area had sprung up overlooking the meadows. Lavish homes began to appear as the wealthy moved further away from the downtown core.

The arts, formerly little more than an afterthought, began to flourish. The Reno Little Theater, established back in 1935, enjoyed a popularity explosion. By the late 1960s, Reno saw the establishment of the Nevada Opera Guild and its own philharmonic orchestra. The Nevada Art League, the forerunner of the modern Sierra Arts Foundation, was created. A domed and futuristic Pioneer Theater Auditorium was built.

That the sixties brought an end to the small-town atmosphere that Reno had enjoyed since before the turn of the century is undeniable. Public services would be expanded, a new city hall would be built, and Reno would look for the first time at the prospect of building what many were calling "necessary" convention facilities.

But the city's government was struggling. Lacking public confidence stemming from the still-present aftermath of the Wingfield era, city officials found themselves adrift, unable to generate enough support to accomplish even the most menial tasks attendant to rapid growth. Many could still recall the "good ol' boy" arrangement under which practically every lucrative contract in the area had been awarded.

A movement to amend the city charter was organized. The proposal, which by law had to have the blessing of the legislature before it could be presented to the city's own voters, recommended the abolishment of the office of mayor (traditionally the most powerful in the city). In its place, a city-manager form of government was recommended with a seven-member city council, five to be elected from the wards in which they resided, two at-large. After their election, the council would then elect a

*HARRAH'S PRIDE. Gaming pioneer Bill Harrah parlayed his love of classic cars into the world's largest private automobile collection. When the new home of the William F. Harrah Automobile Foundation is completed in 1989, visitors will be treated to state-of-the-art exhibits that will chronicle the history of America's greatest machine. Photo courtesy of the Greater Reno-Sparks Chamber of Commerce*

figurehead mayor from their own ranks to perform the ceremonial function of presiding over meetings and representing the city at civic functions.

In 1962, thanks predominantly to feverish lobbying efforts by the League of Women Voters, the new charter was adopted. A group of local business interests, known collectively as the Committee of Fifty and headed by educator Earl Wooster, met regularly at the El Cortez Hotel to plan the election of a new city council. Surprisingly, the powerful casino interests were poorly represented—perhaps due to the fact that despite the rapidly growing prosperity brought about by their own industrious efforts, most casino owners were still considered by many to be second-class citizens. Said one member of the committee in later years, "They would have tainted the good intentions of the effort by their

*THE MISFITS COME TO TOWN.
During the sixties and seventies, Reno
played host to many famous personalities.
Here Montgomery Clift, Marilyn Monroe,
and Clark Gable pose for photos during a
break in the filming of* The Misfits. *It was
Gable's last film. Photo courtesy of the
Greater Reno-Sparks Chamber of
Commerce*

*REACH, PARDNER! Entertainer
Sammy Davis, Jr., wearing a black outfit
but white hat, practices his famous quick
draw—a staple of his nightclub act in the
1960s. Photo courtesy of the Greater Reno-
Sparks Chamber of Commerce*

*LIFESTYLES OF THE RICH AND FAMOUS. Movie star Tony Curtis hugs Sammy Davis, Jr., and Janet Leigh during an interview with Charles Mix. Photo courtesy of the Greater Reno-Sparks Chamber of Commerce*

*PRESENTING THE SILVER SPURS. Harry Parker of Parker's Western Wear (left) and Frank Bender of Bender Warehousing (right) present movie star Fred MacMurray with the Reno Rodeo's coveted Silver Spurs. Photo courtesy of Frank Bender*

ACTORS HONORED. Actors Richard
Boone (to the left of the podium) and John
Wayne (to the right) look less than
enthusiastic as rodeo executive Frank

Bender presents the annual Chamber of
Commerce Award as the 1950s came to a
close. Photo courtesy of Frank Bender

involvement."

The first city manager under the new system was Joe
Latimore, whose popularity would guarantee his position
for the next fourteen years. During his tenure, the city
would undergo a period of then-unheard-of construction—
the Fleishmann Atmospherium Planetarium in 1963, a
new city hall and a jail by 1965, a new library by 1966, and
the new Washoe County Courthouse, which was dedicated
in 1967.

During the period when much of the nation was
experiencing what was known as a "beatnik rebellion,"
Bill Harrah would open an entirely new tourist
attraction—his own meticulously restored array of classic
automobiles. Despite constant attempts by the federal
government to tax his fabulous collection "out of
existence," he persisted. "He fought them. He simply could
not understand," wrote biographer Leon Mandel, "how
the IRS could interpret the ownership of 1,400 cars as a
personal fleet of automobiles. 'Did they think I was driving
all 1,400?' he once asked."

But with expansion there was friction in the city as
well. Claiming that the chamber of commerce did not
accurately represent the interest of the tourist industry, a
convention bureau was formed. South of town, much to
the chagrin of local casino owners, a new, but vigorously

opposed, convention center was built. Though many
gambling interests felt that the center was too far off the
beaten path to attract many serious fun-loving convention-
eers, they promptly invested in adjacent land along south
Virginia Street just to be on the safe side.

To make matters worse, there were rumors of payoffs
surrounding the city's purchase of the land. Wrote
biographer Mandel, "The responsible agency seems to
have gotten a bid for the land and the construction, passed
it on to the city council, and watched in wonder as the
original amount increased substantially. (Bill) Harrah and
others were convinced much of the money eventually
authorized—perhaps half again the amount of the original
sum—went to some members of the council." Said Bill
Harrah, "George Carr, he got a big chunk of money (I don't
know exactly how much). It was common knowledge, for
among my crowd of people it was no secret at the time, but
nobody wanted to do anything about it. I thought 'If
nobody else cares, I don't want to get in where I have to
look over my shoulder when I walk home at night.'"

But despite the suggested growth southward, the
casino interests were still bullish on the downtown core, to
which gambling had been restricted since the fifties. In
1964 six downtown properties—the Colony, Harold's Club,
the Horseshoe, the Nevada Club, the Prim, and Poor

*A HIGH RIDIN' HOWDY! Chamber of Commerce President Roy Powers climbed aboard a giant bull as Reno welcomed its first official livestock event in November 1965. Photo courtesy of Roy Powers*

Pete's—ponied up $100,000 to repair the ancient Reno arch across the entry to a now rapidly fading business district. The new structure which boasted "more lights than all that twinkle in the sky," seemed to be evidence of a decade of new prosperity.

There were setbacks, of course. In 1966 the government closed its facilities at Stead Air Force Base and the results were dramatic. Wrote historian James Rowley, "It caused thousands to leave the city and a drop of $34 million in retail sales during the first year."

To the rescue came Bill Lear, an industrial inventor, who was convinced that the future of modern commercial aviation hinged upon new, smaller lightweight aircraft. In 1968, amidst cries that the city was so anxious to attract an industrialist of Lear's caliber that they were literally "giving the place away," Lear bought thirty-five hundred acres of the abandoned facility and established Lear

Industries. But when he announced that he was also considering the development of a steam automobile, residents relaxed. They were certain that finally light industry had at long last begun to focus its attention on Reno.

In the area of public services, much of the state and particularly Reno still left a lot to be desired. Wrote James W. Hulse in *Forty Years in the Wilderness,* "(Nevada) had the highest crime rate and the highest suicide rate in the nation, but it had no mental health clinics and only a single understaffed mental health hospital. Its state prisons and its orphans' home were badly overcrowded and its health and welfare services were at a primitive level." Although Hulse took into account the incredible amount of transiency that was beginning to pour into Reno, he concluded, "But even allowing for the fact that the statistics on crime, welfare, and social practices are distorted by the unusual economy that has emerged, the

*NOT GOLDWATER COUNTRY.... Reno Democrats rolled out the banners and the red carpet in support of Lyndon Johnson for the presidency in 1964. Photo courtesy of the Nevada Historical Society*

consequences for the educational, social, and correctional institutions are no less serious. Nevadans generally are not more disposed toward antisocial behavior than their compatriots, but their favored industry almost certainly attracts social problems along with gamblers' money."

Although the situation was well known, little was being done to rectify it. As early as 1955, writer Albert Deutsch had blasted Nevada in an article for *Colliers*. While he was referring primarily to the state, residents of Reno (where just below half of the state's population was located) were stung.

> Too rich to accept normal taxes, too poor to maintain its institutions and agencies on a decent twentieth century level, coddling known racketeers and making them respectable by legalizing their operations, while turning a cold poormaster's eye to its poor, its sick, its socially misshapen...
>     There are, of course, many good people in Nevada, concerned about the deplorable neglect of child and adult unfortunates, and wanting to do something about it. But they don't see the effective health and welfare policies of the gambling state, nor have they been able to modify it much—as yet. An awakened citizenry will someday take into account the human costs of the gambling economy and act upon it, building up the vast potentials of this fabulously beautiful state.

Still, the gambling industry had been trying to clean up its act and its image. Under the administration of Paul Laxalt, two large casinos had been closed in the south— reinforcing the belief that Nevada was indeed trying to change. In the north, a twelve-part series of articles

appeared in the newspapers (and were paid for by the Las Vegas Nevada Resort Association) that explained, for the first time, many of the financial procedures of gambling and even some of the problems. It was the first time the casino industry had been so candid.

There were other happenings of great significance as well. Several years before, the famous case of the *Tax Commission vs. Hicks* confirmed the legal principle that gambling in Nevada was a tolerated nuisance and, as such, casinos were not entitled to trial proceedings *de novo*. In his decision, Justice Charles Merrill declared:

> For gambling to take its place as a lawful enterprise in Nevada it is not enough that this state has named it lawful. We have but offered it the opportunity for lawful existence. The offer is a risky one, not only for the people of this state, but for the entire nation. Organized crime must not be given refuge here through the legitimatizing of one of its principal sources of income. Nevada gambling, if it is to succeed as a lawful enterprise, must be free from the criminal and corruptive taint acquired by gambling beyond our borders. If this is to be accomplished not only must the operation of gambling be carefully controlled, but the character and background of those who would engage in gambling in this state must be carefully scrutinized.

Enter Howard Hughes, mysteriously.

In 1966 the entire ninth floor of the Desert Inn had been rented by advance men, and before anyone knew what was happening, it became a regal prison for one of the world's richest men. While many thought it was strange that the recluse had chosen Las Vegas as the place to "maintain his privacy," few doubted that his presence

*JOHNSON FOR PRESIDENT. Betty Sawyer and her children, wearing campaign buttons, pose with Lyndon Johnson in Reno in 1965. Bud Johnson is in the rear. Photo courtesy of the Greater Reno-Sparks Chamber of Commerce*

would do wonders for gambling's tawdry image.

They were right. Before long, Hughes had snapped up five casinos in Las Vegas and one in Reno (the venerable Harold's Club). To his growing Nevada financial empire he soon added a TV station, an airport, and so many mining claims that many thought the mining industry was going to make a sudden comeback. Before long his holdings in the state totalled almost five hundred million dollars.

Residents and politicians alike welcomed the invisible Hughes with open arms. Governor Laxalt spoke repeatedly of the fact that the billionaire brought long-sought respectability to the state's largest industry. Hughes's power was painfully illustrated when, in 1973, fearing that the reclusive billionaire was no longer in command of his empire, Governor Mike O'Callaghan flew all the way to England to interview him in a darkened London bedroom, while many in the nation's press scoffed, "The mountain had gone to Mohammed."

Nonetheless, regardless of the eccentricities, the presence of a man of Hughes's caliber did much for the image of Nevada (and especially for Reno and Las Vegas, its two largest cities). Reno itself would benefit immensely when, in 1967, the legislature was quarreling over the advisability of establishing a medical school at the University of Nevada-Reno. In his typical fashion, Hughes turned the tide by pledging to UNR $300,000 a year for twenty years—the medical school was born.

Hughes's presence in Nevada made publicly held corporations, which had previously shunned gambling, sit up and take notice. Hot on his heels came such giants as MGM, the Hilton Hotels, and Holiday Inns—encouraged by Laxalt's promises that gambling licenses could easily be obtained by conglomerates. In Reno, Bill Harrah, whose properties in the city and Lake Tahoe had long been touted as models of honesty, went public as well.

As the sixties came to a close, the road to further expansion was now paved with respectability.

*NIXON TAKES A STAND. Richard Nixon shares a press conference with Governor Paul Laxalt as the decade of the seventies begins. Photo courtesy of the Greater Reno-Sparks Chamber of Commerce*

*"GRAND" GETS NEW MEANING. In
1978 Reno was anxiously awaiting the
Grand Opening of MGM's Grand, billed as
the largest casino in the world. The massive
structure seemed to indicate that a new era
of prosperity had begun. Photo courtesy of
the Greater Reno-Sparks Chamber of
Commerce*

# CHAPTER 14

# To Grow Or Not To Grow

There were some big events in the 1970s. In 1976 the nation's Bicentennial was celebrated lavishly over three days—with fireworks at Mackay Stadium, a huge parade in Sparks ("Many people were attired in red, white and blue," wrote the *Journal*), and a VFW picnic at Bowers Mansion. Throughout the meadows, there was a contagious festive mood. In Reno there was a community breakfast and the city coordinated a ringing of its church bells.

Three reporters for the *Gazette-Journal* won a Pulitzer Prize in 1977. Warren Larude, Norm Cardoza, and Foster Church (working as a team) snared the prestigious award for editorial reporting and the city celebrated again with pride. "Who says we're a bunch of hicks out here?" was heard often. To locals, it mattered little that the award was given for seventeen editorials analyzing the life and times of Joe Conforte, Reno's most famous bordello operator. The past it seemed could not be eluded, even though cloaked in prestige.

The decade had seen the painful end to the Vietnam War and the embarassing resignation of a president, but in Reno the emphasis was on growth and a new era of prosperity.

"Reno Hits the Big Time!" was the headline on May 4, 1978. "Thousands crowd plush, glittering MGM gaming palace!" A Las Vegas-style casino had finally come to Reno, and the entire town was in an uproar. While downtown gambling interests worried openly that the new sprawling casino with its massive tower would signal the end to the controlled profitability of the city's Redline District, cab drivers, airline and bus companies wrung their hands with glee. While old-timers shook their heads sadly, newer residents flocked into the MGM for a glimpse of what many now believed was the area's finest tourist attraction.

"One moment you were in Reno, the next in Las Vegas," wrote reporter Pat O'Driscoll. "Walking through the MGM Grand Hotel-Reno's glittery front entrance Wednesday night gave you that feeling, something like being in a Twilight Zone time and space warp.

"The plush, red-and-gold decor and those massive crystal chandeliers had Vegas big-time gambling written

all over them on the night of the $131 million resort's gala coming out party."

O'Driscoll had anticipated the Biggest Little City's reaction to the newcomer:

As expected, a sizeable part of the Reno area's populace turned out to ooh and aah at MGM's opulent new adult playground. Thousands of curious sightseers rubbed elbows with serious high-rollers and the Reno community's own tuxedoed and gowned VIP's in a spectacle akin to a Bagdad marketplace.

Here and there, the paths of three groups crossed—gambling "merchants," black-tie "elite," and hordes of "common folks," all flowing through the mirrored halls of the largest casino in the world.

The world had come to Reno. The MGM was not "just another casino," it was a "palace." It didn't have just the world's largest gaming area (It's bigger than a football field!), it seemed to have the world's largest everything—showroom, stage, shopping arcade, even a bowling alley and a jai alai fronton.

Pat O'Driscoll remarked: "Persons fortunate enough to get an invitation to the official 'gala party' thrown by MGM's top executives were wined and dined in a manner delightfully new to the homespun, boots-and-bourbon image of the self-proclaimed World's Biggest Little City. Business people, lawyers, doctors, politicians, journalists and many more gathered outside the doors of the Grand Ballroom. The chosen couples were escorted to their places in the vast chandeliered room, where ageless Harry James and his orchestra played."

Tradition demands that with the opening of any new gambling house, contingents from the competition show up—to make a token throw of the dice, to lay a hundred-dollar bill on a 21 table. They were there, of course, but this grand opening was different. Here for the first time was a new kind of competitor—an entity so huge, so lavish, so powerful, that it seemed to overshadow the very city itself.

THE RIVERSIDE CHANGES HANDS—AGAIN. By 1980 popular gambler Jessie Beck had turned the venerable Riverside Hotel over to another gaming pioneer, Pick Hobson. Arm wrestling championships shared the billing with the Woo Woo Stevens Show. Photo courtesy of the Greater Reno-Sparks Chamber of Commerce

*A HOLIDAY ON THE RIVER. By the late 1970s, the new Holiday Hotel, featuring a dazzling lighted facade, had sprung up along the Truckee River. Photo courtesy of the Greater Reno-Sparks Chamber of Commerce*

This wasn't just another small-time gambler cutting in on the territory, it was a conglomerate. Politicians took notice (Governor Mike O'Callaghan shared a table with MGM President Jack Pieper).

During the previous two years, as the giant metro monolith had begun to rise majestically from the valley floor, other casino interests were making plans of their own. Hot on the heels of Bill Harrah's downtown expansion came the Eldorado in 1973, the Holiday Inn and the Reef in 1974, and the Sundowner and Fitzgerald's in 1975. Residents were finally convinced that Las Vegas had truly come to Reno when another Vegas property, the Circus Circus, placed a gigantic clown right on the edge of

the city's main thoroughfare and confidently opened its doors. Locals wrote scathingly of the garish pink facade. Privately, they boasted to visitors of "fantastic room rates!"

On June 30, 1978, the Sahara-Reno (only one of five casinos to open in a year that included construction of the Colonial, the Comstock, and the Onslow) held a gala grand opening. Ironically, the event was overshadowed by the death of Bill Harrah. The grief was universal, and it buried the Sahara's opening celebration in the headlines. Wrote Harrah's biographer Mandel, "Harrah would have been delighted that in death he had not only helped his own company at a critical moment (his life insurance

*AN AIRPLANE! ON STAGE? The cast of the long-running musical extravaganza* Hello, Hollywood, Hello! *prepares to board a real jetliner that appears right on the stage at the MGM Grand. Photo courtesy of the Greater Reno-Sparks Chamber of Commerce*

*NORTH OF THE TRACKS? NEVER! Doomsayers were predicting that no large hotel-casino could make a go of things north of the railroad tracks. The Eldorado proved them wrong. Photo courtesy of the Greater Reno-Sparks Chamber of Commerce*

*THE RAILS RETURN TO THE RAIL CITY. A facelift for Sparks includes a prominent place for a vintage locomotive, an integral part of the city's colorful past.*

*Overlooking the railroad display is the newly completed tower of John Ascuaga's Nugget. Photo courtesy of Mark Savage*

policy of $500,000 flowed into the struggling company's coffers) but also subverted an important event for a competitor. The irony of his moment of death was reflected in idly chosen words of a surviving executive a few years later: 'Hell, he didn't just feel rivalry, he wanted to bury his competitors.'

There were storm clouds looming on the horizon with the jubilation, for with the growth came new realizations of the ever-present water shortage in the Meadows.

Wrote author James Hulse:

The whole system of ground rules began to collapse. The population growth in the Reno area started to outstrip the water supply available for municipal purposes in drier years. The middle of the '70s brought the most severe two-year drought since the 1930's. And to complicate matters further, in 1973, lawyers for the United States tried to reopen the Orr Ditch case (a suit brought by the Paiutes of Pyramid Lake) on the grounds that the Indians' interests had not been properly represented in the 1913-1914 lawsuit. The federal government brought suit against 17,000 people who had actual or potential water rights along the river.

Hulse's concerns were more than justified. The fragile Truckee River, fed by the melting snows draining into Lake Tahoe, was the plumbing system that fed the entire basin. As the river dropped from the mountaintop, a number of new spigots were being turned on—the property owners of Lake Tahoe and Reno, ranchers and farmers, utility companies, the Tahoe-Carson Irrigation District, and the Reservation at Pyramid Lake. All were clamoring for more water.

Between the years of 1950 and 1980, the permanent population of the Lake Tahoe basin had doubled and growth in the Reno area was only a short distance behind. Wrote Hulse, "During the dry years of the 1970's Reno residents were asked to conserve water in their homes and gardens to assure an adequate supply for the following year, but almost simultaneously the City Council approved the construction of additional hotel-casinos to accommodate more tourists." He continued sadly, "The request for conservation apparently backfired, as a number of residents wrote letters to the editors of the local newspapers, refusing to conserve as long as the local governments were allowing commercial expansion to continue virtually uncontrolled. To Hulse, the region's arrogant refusal to conserve was disastrous. "How did the driest state in the Union, long notorious for its interminable expanses of desert waste, find the water to sustain a seven-fold increase in population?" he asked. The answer was, it didn't.

And the reason, as always, was money. To many Nevadans, torn between expansion and conservation, the

WHAT'S THIS GAME? This interested character is not really a blackjack player. He is one of the stars of the annual Hereford Bull Sale, a popular attraction at John Ascuaga's Nugget. The animals— cleaned, polished, and decorated with glitter—actually appear on the Nugget's showroom stage. Photo courtesy of John Ascuaga's Nugget

THE GATEWAY TO THE WEST. By the late 1970s, light industry was fast becoming a major force in the Nevada economy. Because of its central location, the Reno-Sparks area was an ideal warehouse and distribution center. Photo courtesy of the Greater Reno-Sparks Chamber of Commerce

choice was difficult (perhaps even disastrous) but understandable. Gambling and tourism had contributed $118.4 million to the state's coffers for the period of 1979-80, five hundred times the amount the state had taken in only two decades before.

The mood was one of expectation as the decade neared a close. So certain was the state that Nevada's largest industry was entering an era of new prosperity and growth that Governor List continued the work of his predecessors by making the state's treasury even more dependent upon gambling and sales taxes. New tax reform legislation was passed.

It seemed to many like a good move at the time. After all, in 1978, interstate airline business had been deregulated, creating yet another windfall for Reno casinos. The number of airlines serving the city more than tripled.

Still, there were some who were predicting that Nevada's dependence on the casino industry was shaky ground at best. In 1978 California sociologist James Skolnick had penned a searing analysis of the situation in his definitive *House of Cards: The Legalization and Control of Casino Gambling.* "The overriding political question (in Nevada) is no longer whether gambling should be legal, but what sorts of legislative policy—what structure of legislation—will enhance the prosperity of the industry." With jaundiced eye he compared Nevada's gambling with that of Great Britain, where gambling was also legal. His findings showed that while the British maintained a social policy that gambling should not be openly encouraged, Nevada was faced with a different situation. Nevada, wrote Skolnick, had become so totally dependent upon the gambling industry that the state was now forced to adjust its standards to fit those of the casino interests and, unfortunately, not the other way around. He warned that the gambling industry contained "the seeds of its own destruction" and worried openly that viable alternatives to gaming must be found if Nevada were to survive.

A few people in Reno were listening. In 1979 a political unknown, Barbara Bennett, challenged the open growth policies of Mayor Bruno Mennicucci and the chamber of commerce. When she was swept into office decisively there was evidence that, perhaps for the first time, Renoites were becoming aware of the serious problems facing their city.

Despite the rumblings that new competition from the legalization of gambling in Atlantic City could seriously threaten the ultimate prosperity of Nevada, the 1979 legislature remained confident. Duly noting the voter pressure in neighboring California from the highly publicized Question 6, the legislature reduced real property taxes a whopping 27 percent, eliminated the sales tax on food, and placed a ceiling on local government expenditures.

The extent of Nevada's dependence on gambling and its unconcealed priorities were evidenced in other areas as well. The governor proposed to add eighty-seven new positions to the state's Gaming Control Board. At the same time, when enrollment at Reno's university was on the

*HAROLD'S CLUB PAYS BIG. As the 1980s dawned, Harold's Club (a Reno original) was still going strong, though the Smith family had transferred ownership to the Howard Hughes organization. Photo courtesy of the Greater Reno-Sparks Chamber of Commerce*

rise, he proposed a cut-back in the faculty—recommending the elimination of sixty-three positions.

Nevada's new tax structure would soon spell financial disaster for the city. Reno's expenses, thanks for the first time to a concerted effort to effectively manage its own finances, were unrealistically low. But stringent policies had come too late. The new law permanently capped the city's expenditures.

Governor List spoke magnanimously that Nevada had the best tax climate in the nation. That boast would soon have dire consequences for Bennett's Biggest (but now more conservative) Little City in the World. A recession was just around the corner.

*RENO (?) OR CANNON (?) AIRPORT.*
*By 1980 the Reno Municipal Airport had*
*become the Cannon International Airport,*
*which eventually became Reno-Cannon*
*International. Airport officials, which had*
*originally planned to name the facility after*
*popular U.S. Senator Howard Cannon,*
*bent under a public outcry not to omit Reno*
*from the name. Photo courtesy of the*
*Greater Reno-Sparks Chamber of*
*Commerce*

# The 1980s: A Rude Awakening

To say that Reno was rocked in the early 1980s would be a serious understatement. Some have claimed that it was the decade in which the casino industry realized for the first time that gambling was not recession-proof.

Just as the late seventies had been a period of almost totally uncontrolled growth, the early eighties would prove to be an ironic opposite. In the downtown area the Mapes empire crumbled, taking with it the venerable Mapes Hotel. If the days of the fashionable Sky Room and its glittering past had disappeared, wondered casino executives, then what would become of their own properties?

The answer was swift in coming. Like so many teetering dominoes, the closures continued. Soon the newer, more garish Money Tree went dark, leaving employees without paychecks just a few days before Christmas. The Gold Dust followed the Coral Reef.

The sense of gloom spread over the downtown business section as well, an area already plagued with competition from outlying shopping centers. The corner of First and Sierra, long a mixing bowl for local foot traffic, went dark with the closing of Pattersons Men's Store, regarded by many of the old business community as a city landmark.

The recession of 1981-1982 dropped the bottom from Reno's casino business. While tourism figures indicated that the number of visitors to the Truckee Meadows had not diminished visibly, gaming revenues dropped sharply. Analysts, though for the most part perplexed as to the precise reason for the problem, predicted doom and gloom.

Gambling itself, the experts say, is recession-proof. Wisely termed the "world's second oldest profession," statistics have proven that when times are hard people usually gamble more, not less, the theory being, "Well, things can't get any worse, might as well shoot the works!"

As the national recession reached Reno and visitors cut back on spending, every phase of the industry suffered. Soon tourists were no longer flocking to giant showrooms; they were opting for the inexpensive cabarets instead.

Rather than spend money on even the town's most reasonable steak, they were, at dinnertime, settling instead for ham and eggs at under a dollar.

There were casino layoffs everywhere. Harrah's, now owned by the giant Holiday Inns, cut an entire level of seasoned top managers. In the same breath, the corporation proposed to sell off Bill Harrah's beloved, but unprofitable, automobile collection until residents loudly complained. (It's interesting to note that the Reno of old with its small gambling parlours could easily have survived just as it had for generations. It would have simply been a matter of closing a table or two and weathering the storm. But this time it was different.)

By the end of the 1970s most properties offered not only gambling, but additional facilities which had enabled them to become "full-service resorts"—lavish restaurants, sophisticated cabarets, salons, bakeries, and spas ("frill" services)—were the first to be hit in recessionary times.

Many high-rise hotels, which had wagered their bankrolls on unfettered expansion, quickly sobered up. Adding to the worries was the apparent continuing success of Atlantic City as a competitive gambling resort. There were ominous rumors that other states much closer to Nevada—including Washington, Montana, Oregon, and parts of neighboring California—would soon legalize gambling themselves. The newly formed California lottery, many thought, would substantially erode Reno's gambling base.

Hardest hit were the casino workers, the front-line troops for more than fifty years. As a new age group of computer-educated gamblers appeared on the scene, players abandoned the table games for slot machines. Worse yet, workers' tips were being seriously jeopardized. It was bad enough that tipping (as a time-honored portion of the worker's paycheck) was declining rapidly as the older gamblers began to die off and "yuppies" openly questioned the practice, but when veteran gamblers cut back on "tokes" as well, the feeling of despair permeated all the way to the city's new subdivisions. When the Internal Revenue Service began to investigate the time-

honored practice (coming to the conclusion that tips were
not gifts but income), it seemed to be the final straw. By
some estimates, many casino workers had experienced a
decline of as much as 45 percent in their tip income since
1975. For a town that prided itself on a friendly gesture and
a welcomed handshake, it was a depressing situation. It
was difficult, if not impossible, for most casino employees
to manage a smile for customers. After all, who can smile
when the household income is rapidly disappearing?

The glittering MGM, lauded only ten years before as
the flag-bearer for the "new period of growth," was
snapped up by Ballys (the giant slot-machine
manufacturer). Eastern real estate mogul Donald Trump,
in Reno perhaps to initiate a takeover of his own, scoffed,
calling Ballys and the city "tawdry."

The recession rattled its way quickly up to the state
level, where by now most politicians realized that
Governor List's shift in taxes was having disastrous, albeit
unforeseen, effects. By drastically reducing property taxes
and shifting the burden to the tourist, the basic financing
for the state's schools was now on the verge of collapse.
When state tax collections fell far below expected levels,
the capitol trembled. Wrote James Hulse, "When gaming
revenues failed to rise as they had done each year for three
decades, the state treasury found itself not with an
anticipated surplus of $33 million but with a $70 million
deficit. Nevada's government—and especially its most
costly segment, the educational system—was poorly
prepared for this eventuality; it could no longer fall back on
property taxes."

In the downtown area, business interests were quick
to blame the situation on Mayor Barbara Bennett's

restrictive no-growth policies. When Bennett left city
government after a single term, the voters were given a
second opportunity to choose another course of action for
themselves. When Reno attorney and councilman Pete
Sferrazza (another advocate of Bennett's restrictions)
soundly defeated pro-growth advocate Jud Allen in June
1983, it seemed evident that the average citizen of the
World's Biggest Little City remained unconvinced that
renewed growth was the definitive answer.

I wrote in 1986:

Downtown Reno is a sad place at dawn. I know, I
walked it again this week. The streets are
deserted as the city begins to awaken from a long
night of partying. Buildings which used to
feature the latest fashions and fine jewelry are
mostly vacant now. No one appears at the
entrance, broom in hand, to prepare for the day

ahead. Crumpled food coupons and cheap paper
"2-fers" glide along in the gentle morning breeze,
congregating finally in sidewalk cracks. On a
bank of dented newspaper racks, an empty bar
glass coated with gaudy lipstick plays host to
4 empty beer bottles among the sticky
circular stains.

For more than 40 years people have been
saying that the downtown needs a facelift. For
more than 40 years people, without much success
or, sadly, enthusiasm, have been trying. Perhaps
now the time has finally come.

In the wake of the confusion, the city's proposed and
long-touted downtown beautification project was scaled
back to a mere shadow of its former optimism. Before the
dust had settled, even vocal attorney Nada Novacovich,
who had invested heavily in an attractive facelift of the

149

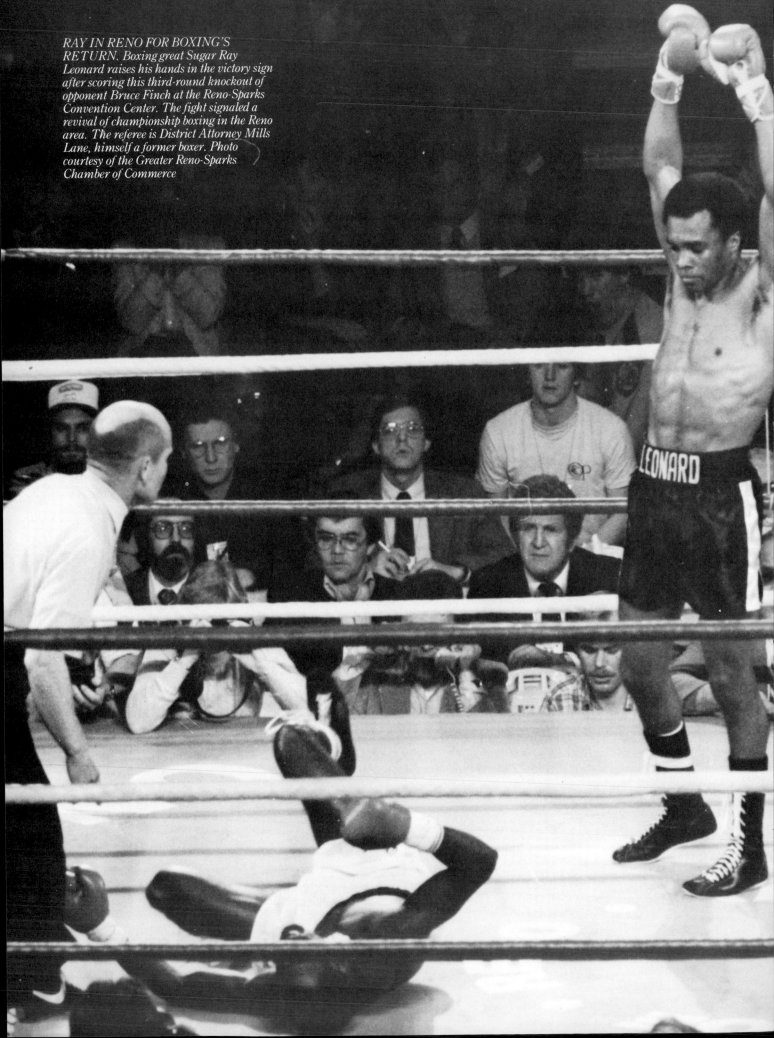

RAY IN RENO FOR BOXING'S
RETURN. *Boxing great Sugar Ray
Leonard raises his hands in the victory sign
after scoring this third-round knockout of
opponent Bruce Finch at the Reno-Sparks
Convention Center. The fight signaled a
revival of championship boxing in the Reno
area. The referee is District Attorney Mills
Lane, himself a former boxer. Photo
courtesy of the Greater Reno-Sparks
Chamber of Commerce*

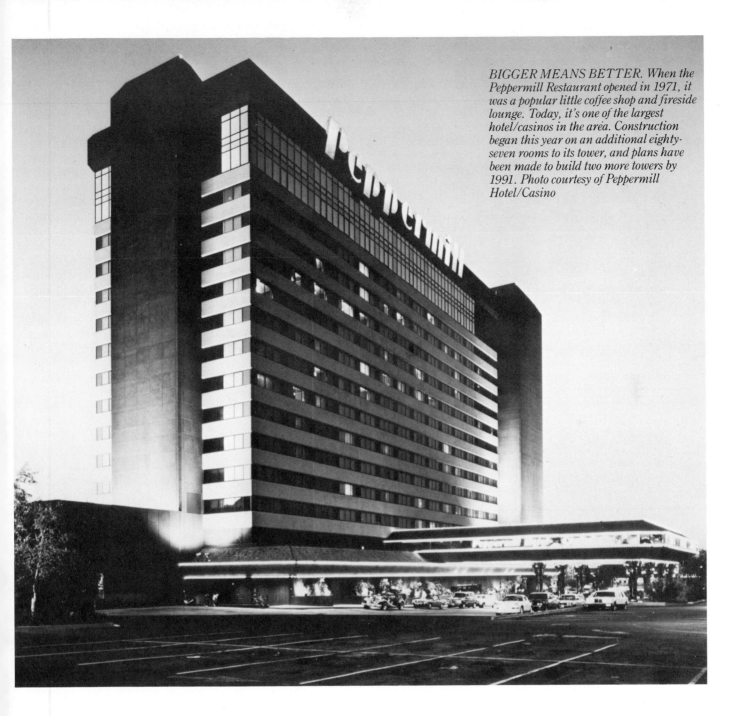

southwest corner of Virginia and Second streets ("This is the busiest street corner in the city," she had told the city council proudly), would see her dream begin to fade.

City services suffered. Short-sleeved patrolmen abandoned the city's parks and sidewalks as the noose tightened around Reno's finances. Suddenly the homeless, no longer wary of a police presence, became more visible. Panhandlers dealt openly in a black market of free drink tokens on every downtown street corner, stopping the diminishing number of tourists with requests for handouts. In residential areas, homeowners were learning that they could no longer count on the presence of a policeman if a burglary threatened.

The plight of the homeless, the destitute, came to light. Although there was little evidence that their numbers were actually increasing, their visibility was.

The governor opened the National Guard Armory when winter temperatures dropped. The United Way spearheaded a task force to study the problem.

Fire stations closed down. Newcomers, many of whom had moved to Reno to retire and escape street crime, pollution, and overcrowding, were puzzled. They encountered an attitude which was failing and yet there seemed to be little desire to change. Visitors who had been coming to Reno for decades were perplexed. And for good reason.

While downtown casinos were suffering, John Ascuaga's Nugget and the Peppermill had been growing with leaps and bounds—giving rise to questions about the need to rethink the city's Redline District and overall expansion policies. There were suits against the city demanding casino growth outside the core. The Reno city council withdrew to sessions behind closed doors, while, much to their chagrin, residents of Sparks were pointing proudly to the "great strides" being made in the neighboring rail city.

In 1987 premier special events, such as the National Championship Air Races, the rodeo, and the Great Reno Balloon Races, drew record crowds. But what was happening to Reno's economy? Why were gambling revenues flat?

To further compound the question, the business community was on a roll. Business interests heralded the arrival of Porsche, the J. C. Penney warehouse, General Motors, and new Pay 'n Pak stores. On the state level, thirty-two non-gaming companies had relocated in Nevada in 1987 alone, adding 1,200 people to the labor force and $22 million to area payrolls. Adding to the optimism, membership in the Greater Reno-Sparks Chamber of Commerce quadrupled. Residents experienced a much-needed glimmer of hope. But when, in 1988, there were three murders in the first three days of the year and even Porsche laid off some of its workers, the sense of foreboding returned. While water experts warned that Reno was headed for its worst drought in decades, locals could not help but shake their heads as more and more buildings sprang up around the airport.

The effects of the recession on the tourism industry were felt universally. Bewildered officials offered every explanation short of bubonic plague—Expo '86 in Vancouver, the sporadic winter snows, the Downtown Renovation Project, which, though slimmed down, was still plagued with traffic problems and lingering construction setbacks.

Some experts now questioned one of the basic principles that had been a bulwark of Reno's advertising since the days of Harold's Club: the image of the city as a "cheap" vacation destination. For decades, the industry had bragged about its cheap drinks, cheap meals, its almost-free shows, and its inexpensive room rates. Economists pointed out that the kind of visitors attracted by this type of promotion were increasingly becoming "cheap" as well.

Comparisons with Las Vegas, which had successfully weathered not only the recession but a near-devastating strike, seemed to validate the theory. While Las Vegas had pursued the "high roller," Reno had prided itself as being the place where the "little guy" felt comfortable—where the "average Joe" could have a good time without "selling the farm." Though many Las Vegas gamblers came by air, the vast majority of Reno's tourists still arrived on four wheels. Worse still, when they did arrive, they spent less.

As the decade neared an end, the economic slump from which the city suffered brought a long-awaited awareness and a fighting spirit from the community. It resulted in the formation of a Biggest Little City Committee, whose mandate was to investigate ways to revitalize the downtown core and to rejuvenate an overall sense of community pride. But pride is one thing and funding is another. By 1988 city officials were pointing to empty pockets and shaking their heads. Under the portentous headline "Coping with area growth," a story printed on May 15, 1988, predicted a 33 percent increase in population by the year 2000. That translated into 35,000 more homes, more than 70,000 additional vehicles on the roads, and almost 100,000 new residents.

Earlier, author James Hulse had written wistfully of the state's precarious position, but he might just as well have been talking about the dark clouds that were looming high above Reno: "Nevada might best be compared to a healthy human who has been well fed, well housed and well clothed for many years, but who is, as a matter of fact, somewhat overweight and emotionally unstable. He has been overindulgent; he has committed himself to too many of the frills over the years, and has neglected to plan for the future.

"Is it," he questioned, "that Nevada has allowed itself to become a kind of institutionalized Howard Hughes, self-imprisoned by the darkness of the gambling economy that has become its fixation, afraid of the outside world and content to live by its own cloistered and distorted values? Is Nevada the victim of a self-induced neurosis that it is unable to treat without help?"

As the decade nears its end, the question still needs to be answered.

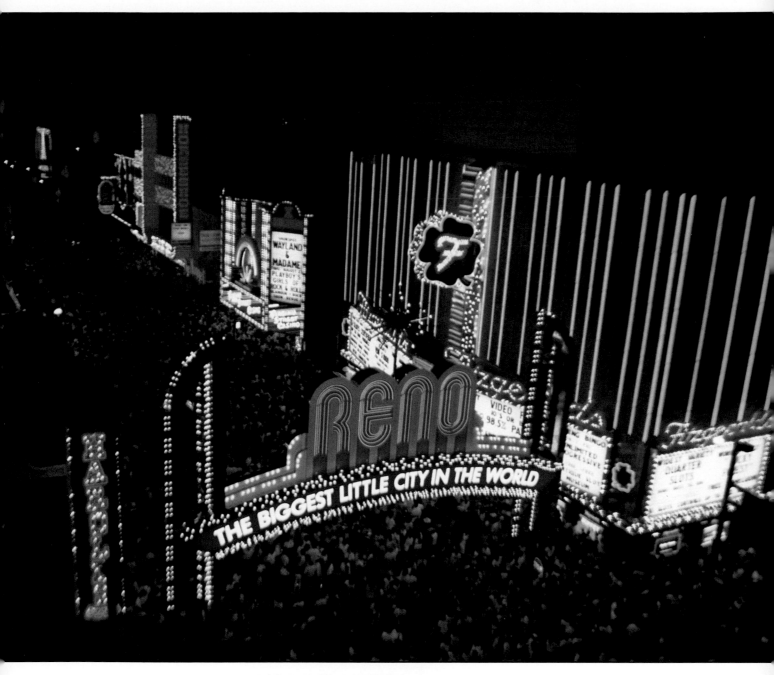

*A NEW ARCH, A NEW ERA. On August 8, 1987, the largest crowd in Reno history to view a special event jammed Virginia Street to witness the lighting of a new arch for the city. For the first time, the marquees of all of the hotel/casinos dimmed in unison—a signal of a new beginning. Photo courtesy of Mark Savage (copyright 1987 by Savage Studios, Inc. All rights reserved)*

*OFFICE SPACE ABOUNDS. The newly completed Southwest Professional Center is a perfect example of new concepts in office space. Photo courtesy of Mark Savage*

*RAIDERS ON THE PROWL. Known for colorful costumes and zany antics, Paul Revere and the Raiders were a staple of fifties and sixties entertainment. Revere, along with partner Bill Medley of the Righteous Brothers, now own a popular Reno nightclub. Photo courtesy of the Greater Reno-Sparks Chamber of Commerce*

*A NEW SKYLINE FOR RENO. In the 1980s the skyline is dominated by major hotel-casino properties. Photo courtesy of the Greater Reno-Sparks Chamber of Commerce*

AN EVER-CHANGING CITY. Reno's growth continues with Dermody Properties' Air Center, a 170-acre planned industrial park housing six major companies, just east of Reno-Cannon's airstrip. Note the housing tracts in the foreground. Residential building has been booming in the 1980s and keeping pace with the area's tremendous growth. Photo courtesy of Bob Davis

# Afterword

# The Future: What's In Store?

Took a walk the other day. Sometimes, it's nice to get out of the car and walk a bit, to smell the fresh air.

But I had another motive. You see, just this past week I have been rereading the most famous novel ever written about our town, *The City of Trembling Leaves.* Penned back in 1945 by Walter Van Tilburg Clark (author of the more famous *The Ox-Bow Incident*), it's about a youngster by the name of Timothy Hazard growing up in Reno. As such, the book becomes a mirror of the city long ago.

I'm constantly amazed how few people have read it, especially since most things written about us nationally have been sadly limited to stories about gambling, divorce, prostitution, or nuclear waste. Those of us who live here know there is much more to the city than that.

We have come a long way in our short history but, surprisingly enough, the things that plague us today are still the issues that have troubled us all along—taxes, growth, and water—and not necessarily in that order. So, perhaps simply to reflect, I reread Clark's popular book. Clark writes:

Whatever else Reno may be, and it is many things, it is a city of trembling leaves. In Reno (their) universal importance is intensified, for Reno is in the Great Basin of America, between the Rockies and the Sierras, where the vigor of the sun and the height of the mountains, to say nothing of the denuding activities of mining booms, have created a latter-day race of tree worshippers. The trees of Reno have regional meanings within their one meaning, like the themes and transitions of a one-movement symphony...the treetops of Reno are continuous, one elevated pampas of stirring leaves, unconcerned with houses and streets below.

Just a scant forty-five years ago we were a city of "tree worshippers." We saw them then as an oasis of greenery. Well, no longer. As more and more of Clark's famous columns succumb to Dutch elm disease, as streets are widened, freeways cut, and subdivisions built, the green—what little we have—has all but disappeared.

Clark admitted he was not speaking of downtown:

There is also, of course, the treeless center of the city which we have all worked around, though not without hearing it several times in shrill bursts from the brass or deep mutterings in the rhythm sections. This, however, is the region about which the world already knows in a Sunday-supplement way...It is the ersatz jungle, where the human animals, uneasy in the light, dart from cave to cave under steel and neon branches, where the voice of the croupier halloos in the secret glades and, high and far, like light among the leaves, gleam the names of lawyers and hairdressers on upstairs windows.

Clark spoke mainly of the rest of the town. Scathingly he wrote, "Reno [is] a city of adolescence, a city of dissonate themes, sawing against each other with a kind of piercing beauty, the beauty of everything promised and nothing resolved."

Everything promised and nothing resolved. I thought about it as I walked along Virginia Street toward the park that bears George Wingfield's name. We've been talking about water meters since the 1930s and downtown cleanup for almost as long.

The problems that we will face in the last few years of this century are the same as our predecessors encountered. To build or not to build. To tax or not to tax. To save our resources or squander them. Today these problems are much more acute. In the hourglass few seem to be monitoring, the sand is quickly running out.

"Where will we get the water?" is a question I most often hear, and we've been asking the same question for one hundred and fifty years. We live in the middle of a desert, a fact almost forgotten in this day and age, but one that was painfully evident to our forefathers passing through. They realized that you can't put up a house, build a factory, or even plant a lowly potato without first determining where the water is going to come from.

To compound the problem, we are not just dry; we are high and dry. Those of us who live here know that the stars seem clearer, brighter at this altitude, that the air seems cooler, fresher. But, as the growth continues unchecked, for how much longer?

Tom Wilson, a veteran advertising man, didn't devote all of his time to promoting Reno; he often took to the desert as well, naming many of the arroyos and hills around here. I can remember him saying, "This country scars easy. You have to be careful with it." He was pointing at wagon ruts, made before 1850, that can still be seen to this day.

There are a couple of interesting theories on what will befall us in the coming years. In his *Forty Years in the Wilderness; Impressions of Nevada 1940-1980*, James Hulse calls for some sweeping changes, particularly in the area of casino growth, and warns "that Nevada already has too much of its economic life tied to the vagaries of a single 'industry'—as it did in the days when mining was its almost exclusive source of prosperity."

Responding to the negative image that Nevada still holds in much of the nation, he wrote that attracting businesses unrelated to tourism is imperative—"Such a policy would demonstrate to potential nongambling industry investors that Nevada truly is interested in diversifying the economy—an objective often proclaimed but then repeatedly undercut by the uncontrolled expansion of the casinos."

He also called for a solidified home front, citing examples of church groups which have traditionally been noncommittal in the past:

> While the [Mormon] Church does not condone gambling and officially discourages its members from betting and working directly at the tables as dealers, it does not discourage them from working in executive positions in the casinos, and there are prominent members of the church who have gambling licenses. Mormon bankers and real estate brokers make money from deals with some of the largest casinos, and because of church policy that encourages every faithful member to give 10% of his or her income to the church as "tithing," it thereby becomes a beneficiary of gambling profits.

Not even the academia escaped Hulse's wrath and he called for a need for getting back to the basics of learning. He noted sadly:

> When the legislature demanded to know in 1981 how all the esoteric research of the professors was benefitting Nevada, the presidents obligingly compiled a long list, which included many indications that the learned men and women of the professoriate were kissing the hands that fed them.
>
> Beyond the churches and the academies there are cadres of responsible people in all the trades and professions who recognize, whether

they favor the [gambling] "industry" or not, that it has gotten out of hand, that some of its practitioners have become too arrogant in the exercise of their privileges. For too long they have left the moral as well as the legal questions to the politicians and bureacrats, who have proven over the decades the Jeffersonian principle that they are not good custodians of social conscience for very long.

Hulse is right in one respect, of course. We have seen the effects of allowing the old warning against "putting all of your eggs in one basket" to go unheeded. The results have brought Reno almost to its knees on several occasions. He is right, too, that other segments of our community—the church, the university, the private sector—all must realize the danger of failing to diversify.

Still another interesting theory has been advanced by Joel Garreau, a former editor of the *Washington Post*. Garreau looks at our potential not with concern but optimism and sees the problems that have befallen Reno and much of Nevada as issues that, with the exception of legalized gambling and generous divorce laws, are not unique. They are shared, writes Garreau, with other large, sparsely populated western states such as Wyoming, Montana, and Alaska.

Garreau lumps all of us into one vast area he calls the Empty Quarter, a region comprised of one-quarter of America's land but populated by less than one-twenty-fifth of its citizens. He views this area as the bedrock of America in the coming years, for the vast majority of the country's minerals (including gold, silver, molybdenum, copper, lead, iron, zinc, sodium, potash, magnesium, uranium, and hundreds of other metals) are found in abundance here. He subscribes to the theory that the true future of this country rests with those of us who live in this Empty Quarter, for we hold the key to the vast underground riches that the entire world will need in the years to come. If Garreau is correct, then it will be ironic. The very industry that started it all, then faded—mining—could soon return to prominence.

However, he warns forebodingly: "There are no futures without water. With water you can irrigate high plains and mountain valleys and even desert to grow food. With water you can create cities of charm and grace in the middle of alkalai. With water, you have wild rivers that charge the spirit."

Garreau, like Hulse, feels a new mindset is necessary:

> As a backward, overlooked part of North America, [the area] never had the opportunity to face tough choices it's having to now. Taming the land was the imperative. Making the desert bloom. Pitting your brains and your back against a harsh nature, and being proud when your brains and back won.
>
> But it's something of a shock, socially and psychologically, for the residents of this land, who in many ways retain the values of pioneers, to be asked to think in terms of limits. If they had

been thinking in terms of limits for the last century or so, they wouldn't be here today. This land doesn't make anything easy.

Think in terms of limits? It will be hard, if not impossible, for most of us weaned on the pioneer axiom that "anything is possible." Nonetheless, we have to take a stab at it. Our very future depends upon it. We have to look for alternative industries; we must reexamine our tax structure and reevaluate our financial priorities. Finally, we must accomplish all of this while conserving our precious water supply.

Up to this point you may think that in terms of our future, I am among those who feel that Reno is going to hell in a handbasket. Quite honestly, the reverse is true. We now have a new arch in place across the entrance to our town and soon it could personify more than just a mecca for gamblers. The timing is perfect.

New York has its Empire State, San Francisco the Golden Gate Bridge. Even St. Louis has an arch (in fact, it has two of them). Reno has always been in search of an identity.

In the early years, no symbol was necessary. Miners hell-bent for riches needed little more than a dream. During the divorce era, it was enough to have the twinkling lights and more than a hint of sin. Even today, Reno's gambling atmosphere has created a place that Robin Leach can still sink his teeth into. To many, we remain the West's answer to "Lifestyles of the Rich and Famous."

For a time the cowboy sufficed. Back during the period when the western was the single most popular form of American entertainment, the Harold's Club pioneers chased the Cal-Neva Indian, the Prim had saloon girls larger than life, and John Ascuaga built a prospector that could hold a Toyota in his pan. Reno, Nevada, was the personification of the wild, wild west.

Today things have changed. And more than just a little. Gone is not only the cowboy, but most of the big-name entertainment, torpedoed by outrageous salaries and cable TV. The anxious lure of Reno's gambling has been tempered by Atlantic City. Here to stay is the sudden realization that we need alternative financing and water if we are to survive.

The place to begin is in our downtown area and, thankfully, that project is finally under way. We've been talking about it for a long, long time, ever since local businesses, only too happy to move to shopping centers closer to the "suburbs," began to relocate. At the time, it was a "win-win" situation. Merchants were able to find more ample parking away from the gambling core. The gambling houses were able to jockey for additional space.

A few of the locals protested. Old-timers grumbled that the town was changing, but it was no more than that—grumbling. And who could complain very much when the town was booming? More visitors were flocking in, gaming revenues were soaring, and more money was flowing into the coffers of government. We were proud of the fact that we could boast "no state income tax." While most other areas of the country were suffering, we could boast to visitors that our property taxes were still among

the lowest in the nation.

Now, of course, the times have changed. The gaming economy has been flat, the resulting revenues as well. People are finally sitting up to take notice. Sadly, it has taken an economic kick in the pants to make it happen.

What will it take to clean up our downtown area? Naturally, it will take money, manpower, and ideas. But it will take something more. It will be necessary to close the breach that has opened up between the downtown core and the rest of the community.

"I never go downtown anymore," says a good friend of mine. "Too dirty. You get panhandled. Even with the new paving jobs and the fancy lights, I'm still a little leery of walking down the street." He's right. It seems strange, though, coming from a fella who stands six foot two and makes the Marlboro man look wimpy. He's content to go downtown only when he has friends in for a visit, and that's all. The rest of the time he won't even go near it. Worse still, there is little pride in his voice.

And he's not alone. The downtown core, with all its neon and crashing slot machines, is great just as long as the money keeps rolling in—money for new subdivisions with new storm drains, money for better streets, money for school expansions and police services. The rest of the time, the downtown area is just "there."

Major properties, which for years have funded university scholarships, museums, and local Boy Scout troops (not to mention such major events as the National Championship Air Races, the rodeo, the balloon races and Skyfire), bristle when they hear that the "responsibility" is solely theirs.

The time has come to bury the hatchet between the casinos and the community. There is no one living in the Truckee Meadows who would not like to see a downtown core area of which we can all be proud. There is no one here who would honestly begrudge the casinos the wish for more tourists, provided that the quality of life can be maintained.

Before that can happen, the gap must be closed. The community must realize that the center of the city belongs, not just to the casinos, but to all of us. The casinos must come to the realization that it's no longer possible to exist independently from the rest of Reno and Sparks, that growth must be managed as well as controlled.

That's why I kind of like Reno's newest arch. The concept has served us well in past decades. The first span came into prominence for the Highway Exposition, long before Las Vegas was even a gleam in Bugsy Siegal's eye. The second arch saw a new direction for the city, the formation of a modern tourism industry. It became the focus of a city-wide marketing plan, adorning everything— billboards, stationery, commercials, the works.

Now, as we look for new direction, the third arch is in place. Perhaps, as we look for answers to what the future holds, the time is right to rally behind it, for all of us to work together. Reno is no longer the small town that many remember, and it never will be so again. But I truly believe that there is still time, time for us to grow—surely and safely—while preserving the image created so eloquently by Walter Van Tilburg Clark.

I am not suggesting that we suddenly leap to bear

arms against progress and development, far from it. Neither am I suggesting a silent protest. Instead, a good place to start might be to pick up Walter's book and read at least the preface—to see what has happened to us in a span of forty short years.

Writes Clark in his book *The City of Trembling Leaves*: "Even from the very center of Reno, from the intersection of Virginia and Second Streets, and even at night, when restless club lights mask the stars, one can look in any direction and see the infinite shoals of the leaves hovering over the first lone crossing light."

I tried it. I walked over to Virginia and Second. The trees are gone now, most of them. Is the sand in the hourglass running out?

*Photo courtesy of Mark Savage (copyright © 1980 by Mark Savage)*

*Photo courtesy of the Reno News Bureau*

*Photo courtesy of Mark Savage (copyright © 1980 by Mark Savage)*

*Photo courtesy of the Reno News Bureau*

*Photo courtesy of the Reno News Bureau*

*Photo courtesy of the Reno News Bureau*

*Photo courtesy of the Reno News Bureau*

*Photo courtesy of the Reno News Bureau*

*Photo courtesy of the Reno News Bureau*

# Epilogue

Reviewing the Reno area's history, one gets the sense of a rugged, colorful group of individuals determined in their efforts to create a great city.

As in the past, our strongest ingredient for success is the determination of our citizens. A renewed spirit of pride has emerged over the past several years that is moving our community toward new horizons.

Entering this era, we face significant challenges that will test our human resources. Growth will inevitably continue in northern Nevada despite feelings of antipathy. We must work to influence that growth in the right direction and still maintain our quality of life.

In the future, new partnerships will be needed between the public and private sectors to bring aggressive solutions to existing problems—seizing opportunities and assuming a continued high standard of living.

Since its beginning seventy-five years ago, the Greater Reno-Sparks Chamber of Commerce has maintained a mission of developing commerce. Today, the Chamber has expanded its responsibilities to meet the challenges of air quality, water conservation, educational excellence, efficiencies in transportation, and other issues that affect the well-being of our area.

The Chamber has always been recognized for being results-oriented, and our leadership role today is more important than ever to the city's future.

From a colorful past to a promising future, the Reno-Sparks area has a unique opportunity ahead of it.

"Reno: The Past Revisited," is not a laurel to our past, but a benchmark to continue its progress into a dynamic future.

Bill Wallace
1988 President
Greater Reno-Sparks Chamber of Commerce

# Bibliography

Angel, Myron. *History of Nevada 1881*. Burbank: Howell-North Books, 1858.

Cervani, Doris. *Reno, A Pictorial History*. Norfolk: The Donning Company/Publishers, 1981.

Clark, Walter Van Tilburg. *The City of Trembling Leaves*. New York: Random House, 1945.

Curran, Harold. *Tearful Crossing: The Central Overland Trail Through Nevada*. Reno: Nevada Publications, 1982.

Curtis, Leslie. *Reno Reveries*. Reno: Armanko Stationery Co., 1924.

Dequille, Dan (William Wright). *The Big Bonanza*. Reno: Nevada Publications, 1974.

Doten, Alfred. *The Journals of Alf Doten 1849-1903*. Walter Van Tilburg Clark, ed. Reno: University of Nevada Press, 1973.

Drury, Wells. *An Editor on the Comstock Lode*. Palo Alto: Pacific Books, 1948.

Earl, Phillip I. *This was Nevada*. Nevada Historical Society. Reno: University of Nevada Press, 1986.

Edward, Jerome E. *Pat McCarran, Political Boss of Nevada*. Reno: University of Nevada Press, 1982.

Garreau, Joel. *The Nine Nations of North America*. New York: Avon Books, 1981.

Geroald, Katherine. *The Aristocratic West*. Darby: Arden Library, 1925.

Glass, Mary Ellen. *Nevada's Turbulent 50's*. Reno: University of Nevada Press, 1981.

Glass, Mary Ellen, et. al. *Touring Nevada*. Reno: University of Nevada Press, 1983.

Higgs, Gerald B. *Lost Legends of the Silver State*. Salt Lake City: Western Epics Publishing Co., 1976.

Fireman's Pension and Relief Fund. *History of the Reno Fire Department*, n.p., 1906.

Hulse, James W. *Forty Years in the Wilderness*. Reno: University of Nevada Press, 1986.

Hummel, N.A. *General History and Resources of Washoe City*. Morongo Valley: Sagebrush Press, 1969.

Laxalt, Robert. *Nevada, A History*. New York: W. W. Norton and Co., 1969.

Lerude, Warren L. *History In Headlines*. Reno Gazette-Journal Publishers, 1979.

Lewis, Oscar. *Sagebrush Casinos—A Story of Legal Gambling in Nevada*. New York: Country Life Press, 1953.

Mandel, Leon. *William Fisk Harrah, The Life and Times of a Gambling Magnate*. New York: Doubleday and Co., 1982.

Miller, Max. *Reno*. New York: Dodd, Mead Co., 1941.

Nielson, Norm. "Tales of Nevada." *Fun and Gaming Magazine*: July 1986, October 1986, December 1986, March 1987, April 1987, August 1987, and November 1987.

_____. "Tales of Nevada." Radio scripts: Nos. 61, 87, 89, 98, 177, 178, 222, 223, 224, 278, 359, 476, 477, 599, 633, 639, 702, 733, 789, 790, 791, 804, 805, 806, 817, 818, 826, 835, 841, 842, 849, 850, 874, 890, 891, 895, 938, 999, 1002, 1007, 1008, 1010, 1044, 1048, and 1052.

Nyleen, Robert. *Reno, the Hub of Washoe County*. Northridge: Windsor Publications, 1984.

Ostrander, Gilman M. *Nevada, the Great Rotten Borough: 1859-1964*. New York: Alfred Knopf, 1966.

Paher, Stanley W. *Nevada Towns and Tales: North, Vol. 1*. Reno: Nevada Publications, 1981.

Ray, C. Lorin. *Backyard of Nevada, A Centennial Edition*. Bishop: Chalfant Press, 1964.

Reinhardt, Richard. *Out West on the Overland Train*. Secaucus: Castle Books, 1967.

Sanford, John. "Printer's Ink in My Blood." Reno: Oral History Project. University of Nevada-Reno, 1972.

Sawyer, Raymond I. *Reno, Where The Gamblers Go*. Reno: Sawston Publishing Co., 1976.

Schrader, Larry. *Reno, Round The Clock: The True Story of America's Gambling Mecca*. Pompano Beach: Exposition Press of Florida, Inc., 1976.

Skolnick, Jerome H. *House of Cards: The Legalization and Control of Casino Gambling*. Boston: Little, Brown Co., 1978.

Smith, Harold S., Jr. *I Want To Quit Winners*. Englewood Cliffs: Prentice-Hall Inc., 1961.

Thompson, David. *Nevada, A History of Changes*. Sacramento: Cal-Central Press, 1986.

Townley, John M. *Tough Little Town on the Truckee*. Reno: Jamison Station Press, 1983.

Wallace, Robert. *The Gamblers*. (Old West Series) Alexandria: Time-Life Books, 1978.

Wallace, Robert. *The Miners*. (Old West Series) Alexandria: Time-Life Books, 1976.

West, Ray B. *Rocky Mountain Cities*. New York: W. W. Norton and Co., 1949.

Zauner, Phillis and Ray. *Reno-Sparks, a Mini-History*. Sacramento: Zanel Publishers, 1978.

# Index